The Pocket Book of
# HOME RENOVATION

D0727243

# The Pocket Book of
# HOME RENOVATION

Alan Taylor

Evans Brothers Limited London

Published by Evans Brothers Limited
Montague House
Russell Square, London WC1B 5BX

First published 1980

ISBN 0 237 45501 3          PRA 7109

Printed in Great Britain by
Clark Constable Limited, Edinburgh

Phototypeset in Great Britain by
Filmtype Services Limited, Scarborough

# CONTENTS

# INTRODUCTION

Do you live in a house that has become too small for an increasing family? Have you bought a flat in a large house and find difficulty with room space? Has your family grown up and flown the nest leaving you with a home too large for your needs and wish to convert it? Do you live in an oldish property and want to renovate it?

If so, this book is for you. Moving elsewhere is fraught with snags and altering your present house can cost no more than moving when you consider solicitor's and estate agent's fees and new carpets and curtains because the present ones won't fit. If you do a lot of the work yourself the money spent will be considerably less; here again, this book is for you.

What is modern today is old-fashioned tomorrow, and so I will not deal with trends prevailing at the time of writing but will rather give *methods* of doing jobs so that you can adapt them as you please.

Think and think again before embarking on major alterations. Make sure there's a reason for every improvement and don't be influenced by persuasive advertisements. The cost of installing an ultra-modern fireplace and new light fittings which could be out-dated in a few years won't add anything to the value of the property.

## Planning and building permission

A man's home used to be his castle and he could do what he liked with it. Those were days when property came before the requirements of horse-drawn traffic and, if a householder wanted to build forward, a country lane would sweep round the construction. It might also sweep round a farmer's acres; and that is why our older roads

7

still retain their meandering charm. The advent of the motor-car and increasing population demand that we consider other people's needs as well as our own.

So, apart from repainting and perhaps replacing old, rotten window sashes with something better or adding a small outhouse or porch without extending beyond the building line, it is safest to have a preliminary word with the local planning department.

These people aren't unduly restrictive; indeed they are very helpful, but they have to consider local amenities, safety (particularly fire hazard) and, in the case of a high fence, whether or not it obstructs the view of traffic on interlinking roads. A fence may not be allowed on an estate with open-plan front gardens. In some cases, even felling a tree needs permission; so may fixing a brass plate on the front door. Your house may be a 'listed' building of architectural or historic interest. A proposed extension may run over an existing drain or sewer.

These laws can be nothing but loose. It's up to each local authority to interpret them, and these interpretations vary from district to district.

Planning and building permission may be separately necessary. With the latter, and while the work is in progress, you can expect a periodic visit from a surveyor to check that the work is being carried out as it should be.

If the preliminary chat is favourable and no detailed plans are asked for, it is wise to confirm it in writing.

Alan Taylor

# 1. TOOLS AND MATERIALS

## Sources of material

Paint and wallpaper shops, do-it-yourself shops, timber merchants, brick yards, demolition contractors (for cheap second-hand building materials) chemists and builders' merchants quickly come to mind.

If you can't get what you want from a builders' merchant, ask for the name of a manufacturer and write to him. Put on your oldest clothes and pay cash, it is worth asking if you get a discount if you do so, to get best prices.

A chemist may not stock the chemical you want. Ask him to order it for you and, if he doesn't want the trouble, again ask for the name of a supplier.

## Tools

Don't invest in a kit put up in an elegant presentation box. Far better to start with the basics and add to them as occasion arises. Buy only tools bearing a name of repute, and store in a cupboard or hang on a sheet of pegboard. Don't forget a lot can be done by improvisation, for instance: if you haven't the right size of countersink bit and the shops are closed, turn one tip of a screwdriver blade round and round in the mouth of the hole you've bored and you'll get a perfect cavity to bury a screw head. If you are minus a coping saw and wish to cut a curve, rough-cut the wood with a panel saw and finish off with rasp and glasspaper. The extra time taken over such improvisations won't matter so much to you as to a craftsman paid by the hour.

No doubt you'll already have most of the tools listed in Table 1. Later on, and as and when required, those in

# TABLE 1

**Basic Tools**

| TOOL | TYPE | USES |
|------|------|------|
| Hammer | Claw hammer | Business end for hammering in nails. Claw for extracting them |
| Gimlet and bradawl | | For boring small holes for entry of nails into wood likely to split and to provide initial entry for small screws |
| Screwdrivers | Two: $\frac{7}{32}$ and $\frac{5}{16}$in tips | Fit the heads of most commonly used screws |
| Steel rule | 610mm or 24in | Measuring and for use as a straight edge. Metric one side, imperial on the other |
| Flexible | At least 3m or 10ft | Measuring size of rooms. Metric one side, imperial on the other |
| Try-square | 150mm (6in) | Marking work to be cut at right-angles |
| Trimming knife | With interchangeable blades | Cutting cardboard, hardboard, paper, veneer, linoleum, vinyl floor covering and upholstery |
| Marking guage | Wooden bar fitted with steel pin and sliding stop | Marking wood to be sawn or planed to narrow widths |
| Vice | Woodworker's portable | Screws to bench for holding work |
| Chisels | Two: about 6mm ($\frac{1}{4}$in) and 13mm ($\frac{1}{2}$in) | Joint cutting and general woodwork |
| Brace and bits | With selection of bits of width varying from about 6mm ($\frac{1}{4}$in), 8mm ($\frac{1}{4}$in), 10mm ($\frac{3}{8}$in), 13mm ($\frac{1}{2}$in), 17mm ($\frac{5}{8}$in), 19mm ($\frac{3}{4}$in) and 25.4mm (1in) | Boring holes in wood |

| TOOL | TYPE | USES |
|------|------|------|
| Surform planer file | Plane and file combined in the one tool | For smoothing wood and soft metals |
| Panel saw | Cross-cut having narrowly set teeth | General sawing |
| Hacksaw | Junior | Cutting metal |
| Spirit level | About 225mm (9in) with horizontal and vertical bubbles | Ensuring that surfaces are either perfectly horizontal or vertical. |
| Wood rasp | Two: flat and half-round | For rounding corners and edges of wood and smoothing end-grain |
| Metal file | Flat | Taking rough edges off metal |
| Pliers and pincers | Former with wire cutters at side | Holding articles and drawing out nails |

Table 2 will help you make a selection. All these are given with a brief description and use. Table 3 deals with a few sundries.

More sophisticated equipment, such as lathe, floor sander, portable scaffolding tower and suchlike aren't mentioned because they'll be used only occasionally and are expensive. Here a builders' hire service comes into its own.

## Power tools

A multi-speed electric drill will speed up work, the higher gear being suitable for wood and general work and the lower gear for masonry and anything hard where the tool may wander from its original point of impact. A hand-

# Table 2

| TOOL | TYPE | USES |
| --- | --- | --- |
| Plane | Jack | Planing long lengths of wood |
| | Block | Planing end grain of wood |
| | Rabbet | Cutting shoulders in wood |
| | Smoothing | Finishing wood surfaces |
| | Router | Inlay work |
| Saw | Tenon, about 350mm (14in) blade with fine teeth. Stout metal-stiffened back | Cross-cutting small work |
| | Coping, with bowed back | Cutting irregular shapes in wood |
| | Floorboard, small stiff saw with closely-set teeth | Cutting old floorboards in situ |
| | Rip, with wide teeth | Cuts wood quickly in direction of grain |
| | Hack, adjustable | Larger work than can be done with junior hacksaw |
| Chisel | Two: about 20mm (¾in) and 25mm (1in) | Joint cutting and general woodwork |
| Oil stone | With rough and smooth sides | Sharpening chisels, planes and trimming knives |
| Hammer | Pin, with small head | For panel pins, tacks and light work |
| | Ball pein | Business end for nails, round end for beating out metal curved shapes, removing dents and driving home rivets |
| Mallet | Beechwood | Closing joints without marring surface of wood |
| Countersink bit | Rosehead, for fitting into brace | For countersinking screw heads |

| TOOL | TYPE | USES |
|------|------|------|
| Hand drill | Chuck capacity up to 8mm (5⁄16in) | Faster action than brace (Table 1), can also be used in a limited space |
| Drill set | Hand drill | For use with hand or electric drill to bore holes in metal or wood |
| Screwdriver | About 10mm (3⁄8in) tip | For large-headed screws |
|  | Short shank and handle | Used in hard-to-get-at places |
|  | Phillips, 1 and 2 point sizes | For use with Phillips screws which have cross-grooved heads |
|  | Rachet | Driving small screws into soft wood quickly |
| Vice | Mechanics | Metal working; with hardboard screwed to jaws can hold wood |
| Spokeshave | Handle on each side | Finishing curves in wood edges. Quicker than rough cutting and glasspapering |
| Molegrips | With lever release | Grips nut and bolt heads much tighter than pincers and pliers. May also be used as small hand vice |
| Cramps | Large, medium and small | Holding joints while adhesive sets; also holds wood strips while sawing to identical lengths |
| Extension ladder |  | To reach gutters and adapted to reach ceiling of high stairwell |
| Bricklayer's trowels | Large and small | Bricklaying and pointing |
| Float | Wooden | Plastering walls |
| Ripper | Medium | Removing damaged nailed roof tiles |

# TABLE 3

**Sundry materials**

| ITEM | TYPE | USES |
|---|---|---|
| Household steps | Folding | Reaching ceilings |
| Glasspaper | Coarse, medium, fine and flour grades | Smoothing wood after planing (wrap round a handy-sized block of wood for ease of use) |
| Waterproof abrasive paper | To be used wet and washed out when it becomes clogged | On old paint - to lubricate rubbing action and prevent flying dust |
| Turpentine substitute | Called 'white spirit' in Britain | Removing grease marks and old polish; also for thinning oil paint and washing out brushes |
| Methylated spirit | | Removing very obstinate grease and oil marks |
| Hard stopping | Weather resisting | Filling holes and cracks in exterior woodwork |
| Soft stopping | Cellulose | Filling holes and cracks in interior wood and plaster |
| Plastic metal | | Filling holes in metal, such as rainwater gutters |
| Soldering kit | | For joining most metals together |
| Wood filler | Generally in powder form to which water has to be added | Filling grain protruberances after planing |
| Cement, sand and plasticiser | | Brick-laying and pointing between brick courses |
| Scaffold planks | At least 230mm (9in) wide and a variety of lengths | Bridging over open spaces |

Also cloths, buckets and soapless detergent.

operated drill is safest for anything brittle such as glass or ceramic tiles where there is a risk of breakage.

An extra length of cable to an electric drill is useful for working on a project at a distance from a power point. Check that the cable is of the three-core, heavy flexible type having resilient sockets and plugs to withstand rough use. The cable-to-cable connector should have a retaining device to prevent its being pulled asunder.

Follow the manufacturer's instructions to the letter. Though an excellent servant, electricity is a savage master. Fittings for the tool include a circular sander for small jobs; though, if not used carefully, ridges will form on the surface of the work. There are also numerous other fittings to speed up work.


# Timber

Timber, or lumber as it is called in some countries, is divided into two broad classifications, hardwoods and softwoods. These names are misleading: although most hardwoods are hard to cut some are quite soft. The most widely used hardwoods are oak, birch, box, chestnut, elm, iroko, lime, walnut, teak, mahogany, afrormosia, meranti, ramin, rosewood, sapele, utile, sycamore, teak and walnut. All these come from broad-leaved trees and have pores.

Softwoods have cells, not pores, and come from coniferous or cone-bearing trees; parana and other pines, obeche, spruce and western red cedar.

Even oak differs from country to country, English oak, being the best, is very scarce and very expensive. Reserve it only for special jobs.

Timber will be stored in a builder's yard and, although stacked to allow air circulation between the planks and covered with a tarpaulin, will absorb atmospheric moisture. These days it is often indifferently seasoned and so, before starting on a project, it is well to put it under cover for several weeks in the room where it will eventually be used to give it a chance to reach ambient humidity. It may warp and twist during this period, faults that can only be

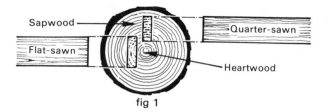

fig 1

rectified by planing which, of course, will reduce overall dimensions. It will also shrink with loss of moisture, shrinkage across the grain being twice as great as in the direction of the grain.

**Flat-sawn and quarter-sawn** Flat-sawn timber is cheaper than quarter-sawn, Fig.1, because there is less wastage from the log. It is identified by wide wandering whorls, whereas quarter-sawn has a straighter, narrower grain, as much as 36 grain lines to 25mm (1in). Quarter-sawn timber doesn't curve at the outside edges as does flat-sawn and is easier to paint because the annual rings are closer together and so fewer stresses are set up.

Grain lines are the annual rings indicating the age of the tree, but these rings may not appear in tropical trees where there is no really cold weather to delay growth. Heartwood comes from the centre of a log and is superior to sapwood which is nearer the bark.

Timber bought already planed saves a lot of time but still needs sanding and is dearer than that which is rough-sawn. Planing naturally reduces dimensions but, for all practical purposes, that doesn't matter. In this book actual measurements will be stated and sizes can be regarded only as approximate. If you use second-hand timber, dimensions may again vary, and that doesn't matter either, provided they are within sensible limits.

**Ready-finished timber** Some man-made timbers are sold for furniture making with sides and outer edges veneered in an expensive timber, or surfaced with melamine. Although available in a variety of sizes and shapes, if they are sawn you will have to hide the exposed edge with an edging strip. Added to this disadvantage is that they are tough to cut and tend to blunt the saw. It is difficult to understand why they're so popular when cheaper, ordinary softwood, planed, sanded and stained and varnished or painted, will do equally as well.

**How to buy cheaply**  The advantages of using second-hand timber is that, apart from saving money, its warping and twisting days will be over; though it'll still be subject to expansion and contraction with changes of humidity.

**Demolition contractors**  You can get good pieces of timber used in buildings that have been demolished from a demolition contractor's yard or building wreckers: floorboards which, when planed and depressions stopped up, make excellent shelves and can be used to make a ranch or palisade fence, and even for the building of a garden shed.

Examine wood bought this way carefully for rot; and if a piece you particulary want is affected only at one end, measure some 600mm (2ft) beyond the infection and pay only for the good part. The bad piece should be sawn off and burnt at the bottom of the garden. Don't use it for domestic firewood or you'll import infection into your home. Watch out, too, for woodworm holes; these yards are nurseries for the pest. Sawing and planing will have to be carried out with caution in case there are concealed nails.

These yards will also stock other building sundries: used bricks, paving stones and tiles which may come in useful.

If a house is being pulled down nearby, ask the foreman if you can have any timber. Here is a source of second-hand doors, not of modern, tissue-paper thickness but real solid ones. In cutting down to size be careful not to interfere with mortise-and-tenon joints. Check first that the door isn't twisted, which will be revealed by the way it closes against the door stop. Where it is already unhinged, hold it lengthwise with one corner standing on the floor and cast your eye down the edge, like sighting a rifle.

**Furniture sales**  Another source of second-hand timber is furniture auctions held at large houses. Some of the furniture is far too big to be accommodated in a small modern house. For this reason, dealers won't bid for it and it will go for a song. Pulled apart, it will provide timber for many projects. Examine the inside of drawers for signs of woodworm indicated by perfectly round or elliptical holes. The back of the furniture is also prone to such worm trouble. If there are a lot of holes, don't bid for the piece; but if only a few they can be treated as is shown in chapter 10. Go for solid stuff only. Veneered pieces are likely to delaminate when sawn. You'll need sharp tools because the timber will have hardened with age.

The joins will be so perfectly glued that attempting to take them apart immediately will only tear the wood. Take out drawers and remove mirrors and keep them in the house. The carcase can be put out in the garden for some weeks – not longer than six or so or weather will change the colour of the wood as well as soften the glue. Once the glue is soft the pieces can be pulled apart easily.

# Fibreboard

Man-made boards have good tensile strength but, speaking generally, they aren't so rigid as natural timber. As against this, they won't warp or twist so much.

**Standard hardboard** The most common of these materials is standard paper-faced hardboard, calendered smooth on one side and rough on the other. Obtainable in sheets of various sizes, from 3.2mm (⅛in) thick and upwards. Use the thinner types for sheathing batten framework of cupboards, and the thicker for light shelves.

**Tempered hardboard** Generally smooth on one side and rough on the other; sometimes smooth on both sides. Uses: for covering uneven square-edged floorboards before adding the final floor covering; also as shuttering for moulding concrete and as linings in exposed areas.

**Duo-faced hardboard** Smooth on both sides for furniture fittings where both sides are visible.

**Medium hardboard**  Smooth or matt on one side, reverse rough. Used for wall panels, chalk and pin-up boards and carpet underlays.

**Pegboard**  Perforated with holes or elongated slots for hanging tools on the wall, suspension units for shelves and ventilation panels.

**Enamelled hardboard**  Lacquered or stove-enamelled on one side. For wall linings, washbasin splashbacks, bath panels and kitchen cabinets.

**Vinyl-faced hardboard**  One side simulates linen, marble, wood grain or pebbledash. For decorated fronts of furniture and fittings.

**Melamine-faced hardboard**  Finish similar to that of vinyl, but is more durable when exposed to heat (but not intense heat) and so can be employed with safety behind the cooking stove to prevent the wall from being splashed with grease.

**Embossed hardboard**  One side reeded, fluted or in tiled effect; also wood and leather finishes. For panelling decorative fronts, such as a cocktail cabinet and similar furniture.

**Insulating board**  Generally matt on both sides. Used for wall and ceiling linings and floor covering underlays to decrease sound transference.

**Bitumen-bonded insulating board**  Impregnated or surface-treated with bitumen. Being water repellent this can be used for making garden sheds or where there is an excess of steam. Hardly suitable for greenhouses on account of naptha fumes.

**Acoustic board**  As this is patterned to increase sound absorption, it does for ceiling linings in noisy quarters.

# Conditioning and cutting hardboard

Sheets of hardboard should be laid flat rough side up, scrubbed with water and stacked for about two days, front side to front, reverse to reverse. They may then be *slightly* damp which is all to the good because after cutting and fixing they will contract sufficiently to avoid bulging.

When cutting into small pieces, use a tenon saw at an acute angle to prevent fouling the face with the stiff back of the saw (Fig.2). Place facing side uppermost so that there will be no undue furring of the exposed edge. If you are using the circular saw attachment of an electric drill, you will naturally have to work in a reverse position because the teeth bite upwards not down as in the case with a hand saw. A way of further minimising this furring of edges is to mark the sawing line in pencil and bind over the line, front *and* back, with 25mm (1in) wide transparent tape, afterwards peeling it off.

For a large sheet, get a colleague to hold it perpendicularly against the corner of a house wall and cut with a fine-toothed panel cross-cut saw (Fig.3). If working on your own, lay the sheet horizontally over four old gate posts, or other timber of similar size. Rough-pin on a batten to act as a guide and kneel over the centre posts, holding the electric saw; then shuffle along, pushing the saw in front of you (Fig.4).

Hardboard can be bent, but if at a harsh angle, soften it first by exposure to steam from a kettle spout.

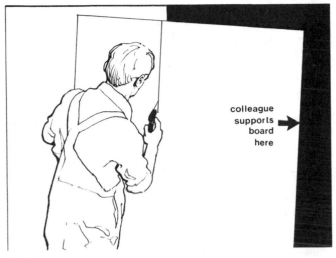

colleague
supports
board
here

fig 3

fig 4

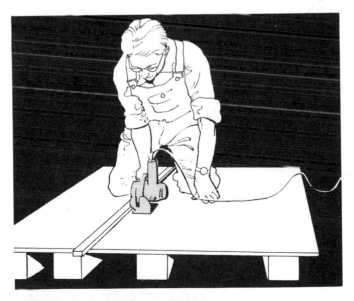

# Plywood

As plywood is composed of wood veneers glued together with grains running at right angles, it is not so prone to warping, stretching and shrinking as ordinary wood. It has three times the strength and is a hundred times stiffer than steel plate of equal weight. An even greater strength is achieved where alternate layers are at an angle of 45°.

The thinnest of this material, three-ply (Fig.5A), is roughly the same as that of the thinnest hardboard but is very much stronger. The multiple type (Fig.5B) is up to 25mm (1in). The former is used as a stronger but more expensive method of sheathing flush doors, attaching to timber frames of light furniture and for the backs of wardrobes and cabinets. The thickest is excellent for weight-bearing shelves, though its outer edge will have to be covered with wood moulding or plastic strip.

Ordinary plywoods aren't suitable for outside because moisture causes delamination. Special exterior qualities may be obtained, however, that are bonded with a weather-resisting adhesive, but even when phenolics are employed for bonding the veneers they cannot be expected to last much longer than twenty years unpainted and when laid horizontally, say, for a drain hole covering.

Cut plywood in a way similar to that of hardboard. It can be bent but only slightly, curvature being dictated by thickness and type, and that is why it is used for boat building. You can also buy plywood with decorated outer veneers. Panels interlined with polystyrene glass fibre or cork improve its insulating properties, and the thicker type is sold tongued-and-grooved for tight lateral jointing, such as with flooring.

# Blockboard and laminboard

Blockboard consists of two wood veneers between which are glued strips of wood 19mm (¾in) to 28mm (1⅛in) wide (Fig.5C). Having these strips only 1.5mm (1⁄16in) to 7mm wide (¼in), laminboard is superior (Fig.5D). When erecting shelves of either blockboard or laminboard, don't

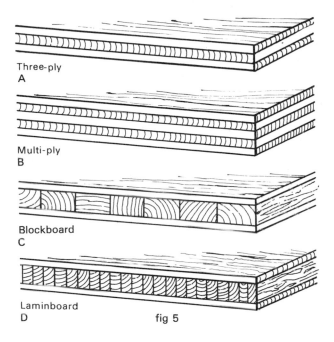

**Three-ply**
A

**Multi-ply**
B

**Blockboard**
C

**Laminboard**
D                    fig 5

forget to have the plain face of an end strip facing outwards. If you want additional strength place the other way round and cover the end grains with D-shaped wood moulding or self-adhesive vinyl strips in a way similar to plywood.

As there is such a wide range of these boards, made from different timbers and having different methods of bonding, consult your timber merchant as to the right type for the job you're engaged on.

## Chipboard

Being made of small particles of wood bonded together under pressure with a strong adhesive, chipboard is tough on tools. It can be bought with rough or smooth surfaces and also covered with a thin veneer of timber. When used for shelves, only the thicker varieties will stand much weight and even these may require an upright support in the middle.

## Mortar

Buy cement as you need it because, even when in sealed bags, it will solidify in moist conditions. Sand can be stored in a heap anywhere, preferably on a flat concrete surface with a slight slope to run off rainwater. Cover with a tarpaulin weighted at the edges to keep dry and discourage animals.

# 2.JOINING AND FIXING

## Complex joints

The main joints employed by carpenters are given in Fig.6.

**A** Corner-halved, here are alternative methods of joining two lengths at right-angles. If the join has to be acute or obtuse, the cutting (with tenon saw and chisel) will have to be carried out at an angle to correspond and surplus wood trimmed off. **B** T-halved makes a similar join in the middle of one of the lengths of wood. **C** Through-bridle provides a more secure fitting. **D** Cross-halved gives a middle join in the same plane, used for table-top bracing and also for cross-membering a roof. **E** Dowelled joins are made by boring holes in the end grain of one piece and glueing in short lengths of cylindrically shaped wood. Before glueing, cut a small groove along the side of each dowel to allow surplus glue to escape. Bore corresponding holes in the side being jointed and insert the ends of the protruding dowels, securing with glue. To ensure the holes line up with one another, blacken the ends of the protruding dowels and impress them on the second piece. If the dowel holes aren't 'stopped' (buried only part way) and are bored right through to the other side, you can align the holes by clamping the two pieces in a vice and boring through both of them in the one operation. **F** Mitred joints need a mitre board to achieve a perfect 45° angle at the ends of the abutting pieces. The half-lap mitre illustrated has a flange on one piece overlapping a rebate on the other and is used for picture frames. **G** Dovetail, used in older type drawers to secure the front to the sides. **H** Boxcomb, hand cutting is difficult and so this join is generally made by special machinery. **I** Tongued-and-grooved, planks are sold already cut to this

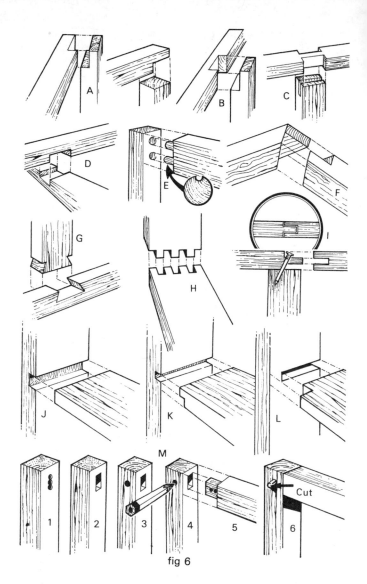

fig 6

shape. A great improvement on the old use of square-edged planks as it prevents unsightly gaps developing in flooring and doesn't cause curling at the edges; dust cannot rise from a sub-floor to discolour the floor covering. It is often *secretly nailed* as is shown in the lower illustration, though this method makes pulling apart difficult should occasion arise. Another snag is that if a floor has to be lifted, the tongue of one plank, at least, has to be sawn through. **J** Through-housing, used for shelves let into uprights of, say, a bookcase. **K** Another version of through-housing. **L** Stopped housing, for shelves when you require the line of the upright to run without being interrupted by the front edge of a shelf.

**M** shows a method of cutting a perfect mortise-and-tenon joint. Bore three or more holes of the required width and adjoining one another in one piece of timber. Cut off the protruding edges and rounded parts at top and bottom with a chisel. Bore a hole to take a dowel through this slotted portion. The mortise should always be cut first because it is easy to shave an oversize tenon to fit whereas you can do nothing if it is undersized. Insert the tenon and mark where the hole comes. Withdraw the tenon and bore a hole in it of the same width as that in the mortise, with its centre not more than 1.5mm ($\frac{1}{16}$in) towards the shoulder. Sharpen the end of a short piece of dowel, apply glue and hammer it through both mortise and tenon to draw the join up tightly. Saw off the exposed ends of the dowel flush. If you wish to hide the end grain of the dowel, sink it about 1.5mm ($\frac{1}{16}$in) below the surface, stop up the depression and sand level when dry. Then you can paint over.

These intricate joints were followed meticulously in the days when animal glue was the only adhesive and that was used only indoors and not exposed to weather. Cooking in a glue pot was messy and made an unholy smell; and when central heating came into fashion, the glue dried too hard, cracked and the joints became loose. That, unfortunately, is precisely what has happened to a lot of valuable antique furniture.

Nowadays there are adhesives for inside and out-of-doors to join almost every type of surface, see Table 4.

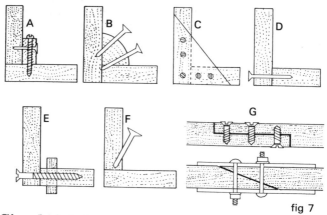

fig 7

## Simple joints

The simple joints shown in Fig.7 avoid the necessity for elaborate cutting and will last a lifetime and longer, though they aren't so elegant.

**A** Plastic corner pieces which can be bought at hardware and do-it-yourself shops. As these are moulded they are perfectly rectangular; once the gadgets are screwed on they will hold abutting pieces of wood firmly and in the correct position. If you don't want to go to the expense of these, cut short lengths of rectangular stripwood and glue and screw to the ends of the two components. But check first with a try square that the pieces *are* rectangular. **B** A neater adaptation is composed of quadrant moulding glued and nailed as shown in the illustration. **C** A device that can be employed where it won't get in the way of anything. The triangular piece can be of metal, hardboard or thin wood according to strength required. Make sure the squared part is at an exact angle of 90°. Then lining up with the edges will ensure the two components being true. Use glue and screws. When screwing any two pieces of wood together, always screw the thinner on to the thicker, not the other way about.

**D** A simple butt joint can be held together by a nail. But as the nail will run in the direction of the grain of the abutting piece of wood it won't provide much grip and vibration may pull the joint apart. **E** A screw is better than a nail but even this won't hold as securely as it should when driven in the direction of the grain. You can, however, insert a gripping cross grain by boring a hole in the abutting piece and hammering a dowel through, cutting off the ends flush. Or the dowel may be sunk below the surface and the depression stopped up.

**F** Tosh or skew nailing. This comes in useful when securing the end of an upright to a solid wooden base already in existence. If the join comes in the middle of the second piece of wood, hammering the nail home may cause the upright to shift; so cramp a wooden block behind it. Punch the nail heads well in and stop up the depression level. There's a snag about this joint; if ever you want to pull it apart, the upright will become marred by your having to chisel out some of the surrounding wood to get at the nail heads with pliers. **G** Scarf joints. Two methods of joining timber in the same plane, the lower is reinforced with metal plates.

## Adhesives

Screws and nails bond two materials by *depth* adhesion; glue and all other adhesives by *surface* adhesion. The two provide a perfect join particularly when reinforced by one of the methods shown in Fig.6 and 7.

Adhesion results from attractive forces between molecules. Not all surfaces have the same molecular attraction and that is why some adhesives are better for bonding certain materials than others. It would be impossible to give trade names in Table 4 because additives are often incorporated which makes strict classification nonsense. Then again, manufacturers have been known to alter their formulations and even withdraw lines from sale. Some are sold in single packs, others in double packs to be mixed together immediately before use. Yet others require the contents of one pack to be applied to one surface and that of the other to the second surface. Some have limited storage life, others last practically indefinitely.

# TABLE 4

| SURFACE | ADHESIVE |
|---------|----------|
| Asbestos | Casein. Epoxy. Latex. PVA |
| Bituminous felt | Bitumen. Bituminous paint. Mastic compound |
| Blockboard and laminboard | Casein. PVA |
| Bricks (interior) | Epoxy. Latex. Mortar. PVA |
| Bricks (exterior) | Epoxy. Mortar |
| Card | Casein. Rubber. PVA. Synthetic resin |
| Ceramics | Epoxy. Latex. PVA. Synthetic resin |
| China and pottery | Cellulose. Epoxy. PVA. Synthetic resin. Synthetic rubber |
| Chipboard | Casein. PVA |
| Concrete | Epoxy. Latex. Polyester. PVA (see page 31) |
| Cork | Casein. Latex. PVA |
| Fabric | Casein. Latex. PVA. Synthetic resin. Synthetic rubber |
| Fibreboard | Casein. Latex. PVA. Synthetic resin. Synthetic rubber |
| Floor coverings | Synthetic rubber |
| Glass | Cellulose. Epoxy. Latex. Polyester. PVA. Synthetic resin. Synthetic rubber |
| Glass fibre | Epoxy. Polyester. PVA |
| Hessian | Casein. PVA. Consult manufacturer |

The prime function of one adhesive may be simplicity in use and of others, durability. Some adhere immediately on contact; others require curing under pressure and may have to be hot-pressed. Some stain the surface and the stain cannot be removed by rubbing. With others, surface stains respond to a damp cloth or one soaked in methylated spirit.

There are gap-filling adhesives too. You can make your own, say, for a badly cut joint, by mixing sawdust of the wood you're using with the adhesive.

The base of adhesives is given in Table 4. This will be shown on either the container label or in a manufacturer's technical literature. It may not appear in ordinary sales

| SURFACE | ADHESIVE |
| --- | --- |
| Leather | Cellulose. Casein. Latex. PVA. Rubber. Synthetic resin |
| Linoleum | Casein. Lignum. Latex. PVA |
| Metals | Cellulose. Epoxy. Polyester. Synthetic resin. Silicone rubber. Synthetic rubber |
| Parquet flooring | PVA |
| Paper | Casein. Cellulose. Flour. Latex. PVA. Rubber. Starch. Synthetic resin |
| Plasterboard | Casein. PVA |
| Most plastics and plastic laminates | Acrylic. Casein. Cellulose. Epoxy. PVA. Silicone rubber. Synthetic rubber |
| Polystyrene sheeting and tiles | Cellulose. Epoxy. Latex. PVA. Synthetic resin |
| Rubber | Epoxy. Latex. Polyester. PVA. Synthetic resin |
| Tiles | Cellulose. Latex. Mortar. PVA. Rubber |
| Loosened veneers | PVA. Casein |
| Vinyl quilting | PVA |
| Wallpaper | Cellulose. Flour. Starch |
| Wood | Casein. Cellulose. Epoxy. Latex. PVA. Silicone rubber. Synthetic resin. |

leaflets. Suppose you can't get the required information, which may be a jealously-guarded trade secret, examine the directions for use and follow them closely. Then, if the product doesn't act up to claims made, you always have redress.

A word of warning about such timbers as teak and iroko which are difficult to bond because of the presence of repellent oils: wipe them with a degreasing solvent, such as methylated spirit, first.

The letters PVA are an abbreviation for polyvinyl acetate. This is water miscible and so shouldn't be used outside except for bonding mortar to mortar, say, a door-step worn in the middle where a thin mortar screed would readily chip off. With such jobs, clean and slightly abrade the worn part with a cold chisel and hammer, paint the surface with PVA and add a little PVA to the new mortar mix.

Old-fashioned animal glues have now largely been superseded by casein which is a similar substance under another name and doesn't require cooking in a smelly glue pot.

## Nails

When nailing anything, play safe by keeping your eye on the head of the nail; then you won't hit the wrong thing – which may be your thumb!

The round or french nail Fig.8**A** is the most generally used and has a serrated head to prevent the hammer slipping. Apart from its unsightliness (which can be obviated by hammering the head flat in line with the shank and driving it into the wood, flat part running in the direction of the grain) its chief drawback is that it tends to split wood. This is caused by the sharp end dividing the grain. If you hammer or file this point a bit flat, the grain won't separate, but break, and there'll be no splitting.

**B** Oval wire nail. This has an oval head and an oval shank. It doesn't split grain so readily if the flat part runs in its direction; but it isn't as strong as the round nail and often bends under blows of a hammer.

**C** Flooring nail. Used for securing floorboards to joists, it also is flat and again you should line up the flat part with the grain. **D** Cut-clasp. Has one of the strongest grips. The peculiarly shaped head enables it to be driven right home with the last blow of the hammer, so becoming partially concealed. **E** Masonry nail. As its name implies, the masonry nail is made of toughened steel or non-rusting alloy and will penetrate most masonry surfaces. It won't bend but, if hit at an awkward angle, could snap; so protect eyes in case the head flies off.

**F** Roofing nail, galvanized for weather protection. When used on corrugated roofs, drive it through the top of the

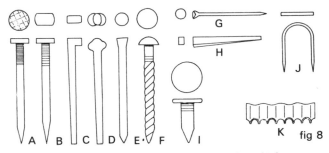

fig 8

corrugation to prevent seepage of rain. Its slight screw construction provides good grip in windy weather.

**G** Lost-head or panel pin. Used for securing fibreboard to an underlying stud, where a headed nail would look unsightly. **H** Sprig. Used for old-fashioned linoleum, enabling it to be ripped off readily. The remaining sprig is then pulled out with pincers. Also used for keeping a glass window pane in position before puttying round a sash and for picture framing.

**I** Clout nail. Has a large head for attaching roofing felt and for securing the ends of sash cords to the grooved sides of window sashes. **J** Staple for fastening wires to walls. Some are insulated to take electric flexes. **K** Corrugated fastener. Used for the rough joining of cheap timber, in box making for example. This is difficult to drive in straight.

## Screws

A selection of the screws most generally used is shown in Fig.9.

After boring a hole to take the wood screw **A**, countersink the mouth (page 9) so that the head is buried. Any unsightly depression left may then be stopped up proud with cellulose stopper and sanded level when dry, rubbing only in the direction of the grain to avoid scratch marks.

**B** Round-headed screw needs no countersinking. Indeed, with the heads arranged in strategic positions, and using copper or brass screws, a decorative effect can be

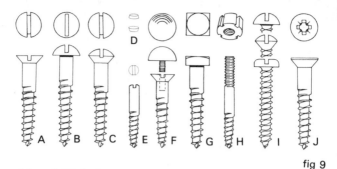

fig 9

achieved. If the longest screw you have is too short to join extra thick pieces, counterbore the top one and again stop up the mouth level, Fig.10.

The raised-headed screw Fig.9C doesn't protrude as much as the round-headed variety and is useful for pieces that have to be taken apart from time to time. The cup or countersunk washer shown alongside in **D** adds to the appearance and prevents marring the surface of the work.

**E** Grub screw, also obtainable in the form of a bolt for securing door handles to spindles, allowing the knob to ride over the spindle. In emergency you can fashion one yourself by sawing off the head of a screw or bolt, tightening the shank upright in a vice and cutting the slot with a hacksaw.

**F** Mirror screw. Used for attaching a mirror to a wall instead of mirror clips. The screw is inserted in a pre-bored hole and a chromium top screwed in. The tops may also be obtained in plastic which merely clip on under pressure.

**G** Coach screw, the head of which can be tightened with a spanner or wrench. When piercing very hard woods, such as an oak fence post, grease the thread for ease of entry into a pre-bored hole.

**H** Handrail screw, the screw end is manipulated with pliers and the piece being joined secured either with an ordinary or slotted nut. When both ends are sharp, that is screw formation, it may be used in place of a wooden dowel.

**I** Self-tapping screw which, when driven home into softish metal, cuts its own thread. A screw, looking

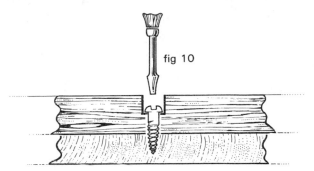

fig 10

somewhat similar with thread reaching right up to the head, can be used with chipboard which is notoriously difficult to join. This is called a chipboard screw.

**J** Philips screw. Needs a Phillips screwdriver. The idea behind the cross-slotted head is that the screwdriver won't slip and mar the surface of wood.

## Fixing things to walls

You can generally determine whether a wall is solid or hollow, that is lath-and-plaster or wallboard fixed to wooden studs, by tapping it. If it sounds hollow then it *is* hollow. If it sounds solid to the touch, then it's built of bricks, breeze blocks or suchlike. Another way is to see if there are any depressions in the skirting-board or base board indicating that it has been nailed on to upright studs. If so, drop a plumb bob from the position of the proposed fixture to the depressions. Then screwing direct through lath-and-plaster or wallboard into the studs is a simple matter. No plugging will be required.

To check your findings by these methods, take the end of a door opening and measure its thickness, less any enrichments. If this is 120mm (4¾in) or more, it is likely to be solid. If there's no door in the wall on which you are working, use two doors on an adjoining dividing wall. Measure the distance between the architrave of one door to the wall, add it to a similar distance from the architrave of the other door and subtract from the total distance

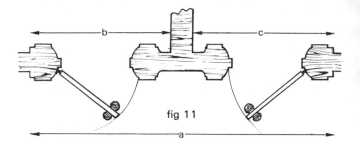

fig 11

between the two architraves. Sounds complicated; so refer to Fig.11 where wall thickness is $a-(b+c)$.

**Wall plugs**   Solid walls may be bored with a masonry bit slightly deeper than the length of the screw you're using; hammer in a plug of wood and screw into that, as is shown in **A** Fig.12. The snag about this simple method is that the thread of the screw follows the grain of the plug, though the process of tightening up should act as compensation. Note the slight space left at the end of the plug to prevent the screw's tip from fouling the masonry. Proprietary plastic plugs with serrated sides are sold and are handier to use. They may be obtained in a variety of thicknesses, lengths and borings. Some are in long strips so that you can cut off what you require. You can also get similar plugs of fibre, though these aren't serrated at the sides. The easiest way to use these plugs is partly to insert the screw in the hollow provided, offer it up to the hole you've bored and hammer it home, then tighten the screw. This is shown in **B.**

**Plugging hollow walls**   It may not always be convenient to use studs for fixing because they may not be at the correct distance apart for the job, say 400mm (16in).

In such cases use one of the patent fixtures illustrated in **C–G.** Such devices will, of course, hold only light items.

**C** Gravity toggle. Here the hole takes the bolt and closed toggle. When the toggle reaches the other side of the sheathing, the longer part of the arm will drop by its superior weight and screwing up can then be completed.

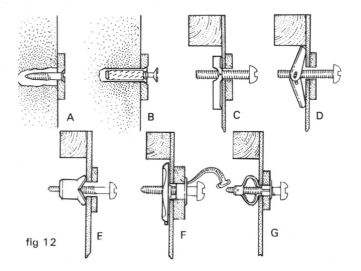

fig 12

**D** Spring toggle operated by two hinged arms which close too flat when the bolt is driven home. **E** Plastic toggle, suitable only for the lightest of weights. **F** Nylon toggle, consisting of a flat bar and thin plastic tape which are pushed through the hole and the tape pulled out while you insert the screw. Cut off the end of the tape flush afterwards. **G** Malleable metal toggle. As the bolt is tightened the metal squeezes flat so making a fairly secure fixing.

**Outside plugs**  Malleable metal plugs are sold for insertion in pre-bored brick or concrete for outside work. You can make your own by flattening a used toothpaste tube with a hammer, cutting it to size and winding it round a screw before driving into the hole and tightening up. The metal will be a soft alloy and it will mould into the thread of the screw and also on to the sides of the hole.

**Flat plugs**  If an elongated slot is required to take a wide plug, between brick courses for instance, use a thicker piece of wood than is needed and chamfer off upper and lower opposing corners. This will impart a slight twist to the plug which, on being driven in with a hammer or

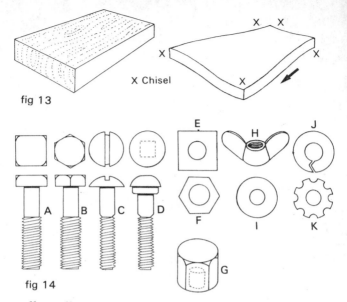

fig 13

X Chisel

fig 14

mallet will ensure a firmer grip. It is a simplified version of the action of a screw, Fig.13. Warm all wooden plugs before insertion to make sure they are dry and prevent shrinkage when in a wall. The plug will then absorb slight moisture from surrounding masonry and swell to make a tight fit.

**Concrete floors** Specially designed bolt anchors for fastening sleeper plates to the top of a low concrete wall may be obtained from a builders' merchant. Used in the erection of home-made garden sheds or forcing frames. The business end of the bolt obtrudes above floor level, is inserted through a hole in the plate and fitted with a nut. You can, of course, use an ordinary square-headed bolt upside down and insert it in the concrete while still wet.

## Nuts, bolts and washers

Common types of bolt are illustrated in Fig.14, the plan of

heads **A** to **D** being above the profiles. Fine threads are for small work and coarser threads for larger work where greater strength is required.

**A** Square-headed (also obtainable with a slightly domed top) **B** Hexagonal is more suitable for working with a spanner or wrench in enclosed spaces. **C** Round-headed, to be manipulated with a screwdriver. **D** Coach bolt. Driven into a pre-bored hole until the square collar beneath the head bites into the wood and prevents twisting while the nut is being fixed the other end.

**Nuts**  **E** Square and **F** hexagonal used where tightening cannot be done with a full turn of the spanner. **G** Domed, where appearance is important, this hides the protruding end of the bolt. **H** Winged nut, which can be operated by hand on jobs requiring to be taken apart frequently.

Sometimes two square or hexagonal nuts are used, the first to tighten the work, the second to keep the first from untwisting. A notable example is the fastening of a pulley of a sliding garage door that is so frequently opened and closed – not always with care.

**Washers**  Help to stop a nut from unturning and also prevent marring the surface of work. **I** is plain and **J** cut to give spring – called a spring washer. **K** Externally toothed washer, the teeth can also be internal. A similar device is a timber connector, whose teeth protrude out of plane to grip work; and yet another for locking a split pin.

# Door and cabinet hinges

Hinges for doors, wardrobes and cabinets are legion: piano hinges which run the whole length of a door, antique and ornamental hinges and secret hinges in all shapes and sizes. Here are just a few of the most common ones.

Fig.15 **A** Ordinary door hinge which requires its flanges to be rebated into jamb and door edge so that it will close properly. Make sure it is mounted vertically or it will work stiffly and squeak. **B** Rising butt lifts a door over a fitted carpet without leaving a gap at the bottom when

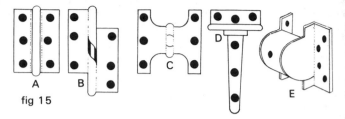

fig 15

closed which will let in draught. As the device starts to operate only after the door is partially opened, chamfer the top hinge-side of the door slightly so that it clears the doorcase lintel. Because of the slope of its working parts, an opened door will tend to close automatically, though the force isn't sufficient for the lock to engage. The socket flange can be lifted out of the pivoted flange without removing screws, should the door need any special attention.

**C** Parliament hinge enables door to rotate to 180°. **D** Gate hinge, for hanging heavy garden gates. Small part is screwed into a post and the long arm into the gate. **E** Pivot hinge, various adaptations of this design are for centrally hung windows.

# 3. TWO ROOMS INTO ONE ~ ONE INTO TWO

The first two chapters have covered elementary workshop practice in brief. Now let us see how these principles can be applied to the renovation of your home.

## Two into one

Methods of determining whether a wall dividing two rooms is of brick or building block, or whether it is hollow, that is, lath-and-plaster or wallboard pinned on to wooden studs, without damage are shown on page 35. But, as you're proposing to *demolish* a wall between two small rooms to make a larger one damage to it won't matter; and so a simple alternative is to drive nails in at intervals. If they go in easily, the wall is hollow; if they bend under the blows of a hammer it'll be solid.

**Hollow walls** A hollow wall won't be load-bearing, that is, it doesn't take the weight of a wide-span ceiling or a brick dividing wall immediately above, and can easily be torn down without interfering with the structure of the building. Locate the position of the perpendicular studs in the wall you wish to demolish (page 35) nearest the two opposing walls. Bore a succession of holes overlapping one another, 6–12mm (¼–½in) in diameter alongside and near the top, and start sawing through laths or other sheathing with a pad or keyhole saw. These are pointed at the tip for ease of insertion in a confined space. Saw a little way down and then change to a panel saw which will be quicker in action. Sheathing and cross noggings and perpendicular studs can be cut through at the same time.

With old property, don't go too near the side walls. It is quite likely that one or other of the two small rooms have

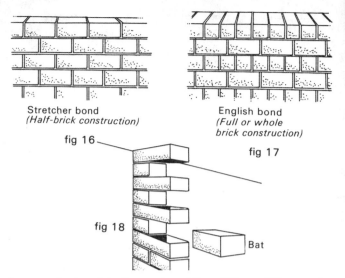

Stretcher bond
*(Half-brick construction)*

English bond
*(Full or whole brick construction)*

fig 16

fig 17

fig 18

Bat

been replastered in the past and there'll be a difference in levels. Even if the walls and ceilings of the two rooms being brought together are perfectly even, a gap will be left which will have to be stopped up with plaster. On drying out, the plaster will shrink and crack and look horrible.

Leave a few inches at least of the old dividing wall and its rough edge can be disguised with plaster. Or you can add plastic pilasters which can be bought at a d.i.y. shop to make an attractive frame for the opening. The gap in the ceiling can be covered with a thin beam screwed into joists above.

**Solid Walls** Long ago, when material and labour were cheap, walls dividing two rooms were often built of half bricks (half brick doesn't mean a brick cut in half, but one laid lengthways in a stretcher bond Fig.16); a whole brick is one laid sideways Fig.17. The former will be *about* 110mm (4½in) thick, and the latter 220mm (9in).

The first thing is to determine whether whole brick walls are load-bearing, carrying a weight above, or merely partitions. Whole brick construction may not apply only to outside walls. Sometimes, when ceiling joists aren't sufficiently strong to take a wide span, an *internal* wall may be load-bearing. Generally you can determine this by examining whether there is a similar wall immediately above on an upper floor; and by lifting a ground floor floorboard and seeing if it rests on a sleeper wall. Then climb into the attic to make sure it doesn't come immediately under a roofing king pin (upright member supporting the ridge of the roof).

Having satisfied yourself that the wall is merely a partition, knock out the bricks. As they will be stretchers they will leave ragged edges at the sides. Trowel mortar on upper and lower surfaces of bats, push into the gaps and plaster over. Bats are bricks cut crossways in half, Fig.18.

Removal of load-bearing walls necessitates propping up while a steel joist is inserted to take the weight of rooms above. This involves a knowledge of stresses and strains and heavy lifting and is best left to a builder who may have to consult an architect.

## One into two

In the past, large houses were built with large rooms, a waste of space for the average family of today. To divide a room into two, measure the width of the room where a partition is to be built by placing two battens on the floor, shorter than room width but long enough to overlap in the middle. One end of each batten should touch an opposing wall. Mark where the battens meet and add together the lengths of both up to your mark, Fig.19. Use this measurement to calculate the width of the room and estimate how many perpendicular studs will be required. Studs should be at a minimum of 400mm (16in) apart.

For the usual size of room you can get away with 50mm$^2$ (2×2in) studding. Larger or wider rooms may need something stouter, say, 75×50mm. (3×2in). Use the larger size narrow side outwards; wider side parallel to the opposing walls, so making the partition 75mm (3in) thick.

Pencil a line on the ceiling with a straight edge or string tied tightly across where the partition is to come. Drop a plumb-bob along this line down and mark the corresponding position on the floor. A 25×50mm (1×2in) batten of length equal to the width of the room, which you have already established, will act as a floor plate, and this should be screwed into the flooring.

If the floor is of concrete or quarry tiles, use fibre plugs and don't bore holes too deeply or you'll puncture the underlying damp-proof membrane. After all, the screws are merely to keep the plate in position and prevent its bulging outwards. Use a masonry bit for the holes.

Now for the ceiling plate which should be of similar dimension, but check to make sure, as old walls can lean inwards or outwards. This will be nailed through the ceiling plaster to joists overhead. The joists can be located by seeing where flooring nails are in the room above, measuring the distance from one to another and to the nearest wall and transferring these measurements to the ceiling below.

Where joists run in the same direction as your proposed partitioning arrange for it to come below one of them. If that upsets your plans, there is nothing for it but to add cross-noggings so that there'll be something solid to take the nails, Fig.21. To reach the joists remove a few floor-boards from the room above by driving a bolster or wide chisel in the gap between the boards where they're nailed on to the joists and lever up. The remainder of the board can then be released by further levering. Cross-noggings may also have to be used if joists run at right angles to the partitioning.

Before fixing these plates, rebate them at intervals of about 400mm (16in) to take upright studs which should also be rebated to the same degree. These T-half joins (Fig.6B, page 26) will ensure an even surface on the same plane at both sides. The *precise* distance between each upright stud can only be determined in relation to the width of the wallboard you intend using as sheathing because, although you can have several studs under the middle of a sheet, there *must* be one under abutting edges. On no account should edges swing loose between studs.

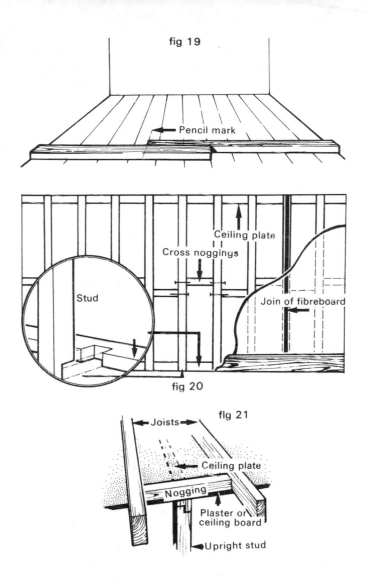

fig 19

Pencil mark

Ceiling plate

Cross noggings

Stud

Join of fibreboard

fig 20

fig 21

Joists

Ceiling plate

Nogging

Plaster or
ceiling board

Upright stud

45

The more exact the length of the upright studs the stronger the fitting will be. As old ceilings often slope slightly, measure heights at intervals, following a method similar to that adopted for floor plates, and cut the studs accordingly. Secure the rebated parts to ceiling and floor plates with non-ferrous nails.

Cross-noggings will be needed at intervals; and for a room of average height, about 2.44m (8ft), one set only will be needed. Anything higher than this requires more. Stagger them slightly so that you can nail through the studs into them, Fig.20.

Medium or, preferably, fire-resistant fibreboard, 3.2mm (⅛in) thick will do for the sheathing on both sides, unless there are boisterous children about when a thicker board may be needed. Condition the board before erection, as is described on page 20. Fill the intervening space with quilted acoustic material tacked on to the sides of the studs to prevent it from slipping down.

Pin boards to studs with lost-head nails. Work from the centre, up and down alternately, and on to floor and ceiling plates and also cross-noggings in the same way, about 5mm (³⁄₁₆in) from the edges and 100mm (4in) apart. One of the adhesives listed on page 30 may be used instead of nails; nothing will then show except the joins which must be at least 1.5mm (¹⁄₁₆in) apart. Paint a creamy consistency of plaster into this gap, press in scrim tape and complete the stopping by knifing over more plaster, this time of a mustard consistency. Sand level when dry and the wall will be ready for decorating. Scrim is a strong, thin fabric which can be bought in ribbon form or cut from a larger sheet. Another way is to poke nylon string into the gap and plaster over. Alternatively you can use cover strips chosen from the selection in Fig.22.

Where wallboard meets ceiling, hide the ugly joins with wood, plastic, plaster or stiffened paper ceiling cove obtainable at wallpaper and timber stores. If you *must* make a faithful copy of an elaborate cornice already on the remaining walls you're in for a complicated job. Remove a portion of the old and make a plaster of Paris mould from it. Seal the inner surface with a coating of shellac and pour in plaster, reinforcing it with wire and scrim.

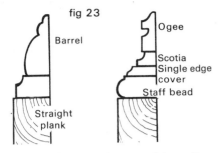

fig 23

Barrel

Straight plank

Ogee

Scotia
Single edge cover

Staff bead

You will have difficulty in matching the easing (ornamental top of skirting or base board) with that attached to the existing old walls unless you get some turned specially. You can, however, achieve as near a match as makes no practical odds by pinning or sticking on to the edge of a planed plank, 25mm (1in) thick, one or more of the mouldings shown in Fig.22. Examples are given in Fig.23. You may have to cut them lengthways to fit. This range indicates shape only. The mouldings are sold in a variety of sizes. No timber yard or d.i.y. shop will stock them all, so you may have to shop round.

Instead of fibreboard as a sheathing you can nail on pinewood, tongued-and-grooved and secretly nailed (Fig.6, page 26). Either stain and varnish the planks after fitting or, if you want a plain wood finish, use varnish only, alternating matt and gloss and finishing up with the surface you want. Varnish makes cleaning easier because it offers less resistance to the rubbing action of the cleaning cloth and it doesn't attract dust readily.

**Door** It is better not to make provision for communication between the two new rooms. Fitting a door presents problems, slamming it could disturb the studding and, if the television or children are in one room, there will be a lot of sound transference to the other. Far better to make entries and exits through doors already in existence. If, however, a communicating door is essential, buy the door first and leave it in the room for some weeks to achieve ambient humidity. The studs in the immediate vicinity will have to be so arranged and cut that a doorcase of the

47

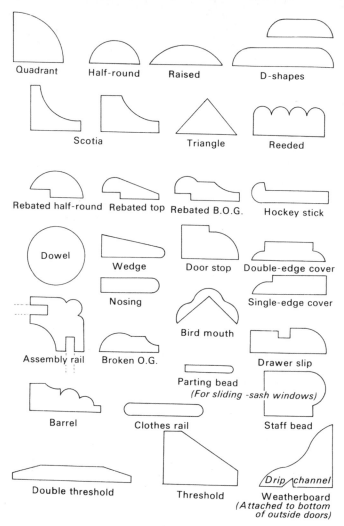

Quadrant

Half-round

Raised

D-shapes

Scotia

Triangle

Reeded

Rebated half-round

Rebated top

Rebated B.O.G.

Hockey stick

Dowel

Wedge

Door stop

Double-edge cover

Nosing

Single-edge cover

Assembly rail

Broken O.G.

Bird mouth

Drawer slip

Parting bead
*(For sliding-sash windows)*

Barrel

Clothes rail

Staff bead

Double threshold

Threshold

Drip channel

Weatherboard
*(Attached to bottom of outside doors)*

fig 22

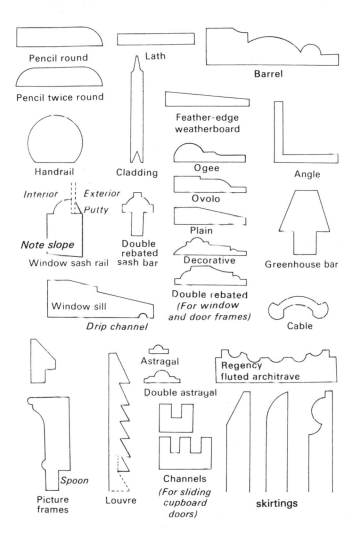

Pencil round

Pencil twice round

Lath

Barrel

Handrail

Cladding

Feather-edge weatherboard

Ogee

Angle

*Interior*   *Exterior*

*Putty*

*Note slope*

Window sash rail

Double rebated sash bar

Ovolo

Plain

Decorative

Greenhouse bar

Window sill

*Drip channel*

Double rebated
*(For window
and door frames)*

Cable

Astragal

Double astragal

Regency
fluted architrave

*Spoon*

Picture
frames

Louvre

Channels
*(For sliding
cupboard
doors)*

skirtings

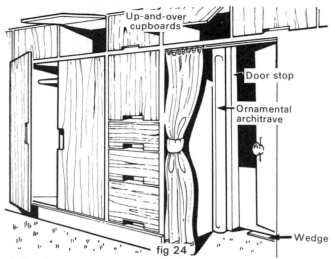

Labels in figure: Up-and-over cupboards · Door stop · Ornamental architrave · Wedge · fig 24

right dimensions can be built. You won't be able to increase the thickness of the studs so nail boards of width equal to the *total* thickness of the partition to the studs at top and at two sides. Punch in nail heads and stop up level ready for painting.

An ornamental architrave may be added to act as a frame. Choose one from those in Fig.22.

Now hang the door, recessing the hinges and making sure it's vertical by checking with a spirit level. Wedge up the bottom slightly so that it does not foul the floor and get a colleague to hold it in this position when closed. Attach stops, thin wood strips against which the door closes, with finger pressure against them while you nail them on making the fitting sufficiently tight to exclude draughts but not so that coats of paint will cause jamming, Fig.24.

If one of the rooms is used for living in and the other for sleeping, considerable sound transference can be muffled by building fittings on the bedroom side, the whole length and height of the partition. These could comprise wardrobes and drawers and could be some 560mm (22in) in depth, saving space and the expense of free standing units. The clothes will make excellent sound insulation.

# 4. ADDING A ROOM

Adding a prefabricated wooden extension to a house destroys its external appearance. The writer has examined many and in all cases they have not fulfilled the expectations raised by their advertisements. In some there have been serious faults. Weak or total absence of flashing to run rainwater off the house walls on to the roof of the lean-to; a flat roof insufficiently strong to bear the weight of a man and ladder for reaching a window or guttering immediately above; lack of insulation; insubstantial doors, these are but a few. Their advantages are that they may be a third or a quarter of the price of a brick-built addition and can be erected in a few days.

The ideal is to use bricks, employing a builder who specialises in such work and knows from experience the snags likely to be encountered such as joining up new bricks with old, making allowances for uneven walls and arranging for adequate ventilation. He should also be able to arrange for the necessary plans to submit for approval.

## Attic room

Roofs built in the early part of this century and before are steeply pitched for rain to escape quickly. That was in the days before interlocking tiles which allow for less water penetration and before the cost of materials and labour started to soar.

The space below an old steeply-pitched roof is wasted and can be turned into an extra room. This again is a job for a builder; but here are a few pointers to indicate what is involved.

**Stairs** The first thing to be considered is where stairs

leading to the attic can be fitted. They must be of permanent design and can be bought ready-made or constructed to your specification by a carpenter following the principles given on page 79. If the room is going to be lived in, as a bedroom perhaps, the stairs should be lined with fire-resisting sheeting nailed underneath treads and risers. Movable loft ladders are usually only used when the top is used for storage purposes. Ideally there will be space for the foot of the new stairs on the landing below. If not, the size of one of the existing bedrooms will have to be sacrificed, the space underneath being utilised as a fitted wardrobe and cupboards.

A ranch-type stair rail is shown in Fig.25 and it is assumed there will be a protective wall on the other side. This illustration also indicates the top of the stairs obtruding through an aperture in the floor of the attic. A trap door would be heavy to lift and take up valuable time in emergencies. It would also prevent heat rising from the main body of the house in cold weather and make the room too warm in hot weather. It would be better to fit a gateway at the top of the stairs, or erect a partition between stairs and room with a door which can be left open when required.

**Strengthening joists**  Ceiling joists will have to be cut to allow for access, and the cut parts joined up with cross-noggings and strengthened, see Fig.25. Other joists may also need strengthening or adding to to carry the additional weight of furniture. See Tables 5 and 6, page 58.

As an alternative to floorboards, a thick gauge of chipboard (page 23) may be cut down in size so that you can get it through the aperture in the attic floor.

Lay some of this flooring temporarily so that you don't put your foot through the ceiling below.

**Windows**  Knocking out bricks in a gable is the obvious solution to the problem of a window, Fig.26C. But if, for any reason, a window cannot be fixed in this position you will have to resort to roof lighting, Fig.27, and one that pivots in the middle will be easiest to clean. This will

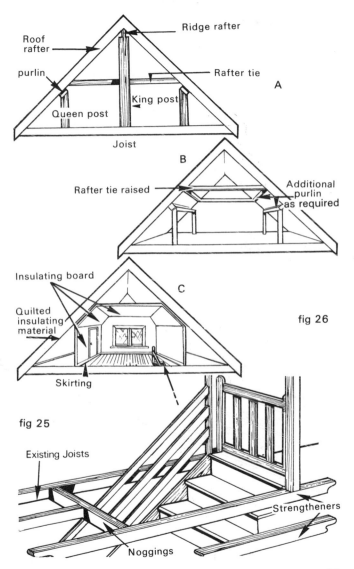

Ridge rafter

Roof rafter

purlin

Rafter tie

King post

Queen post

Joist

A

B

Rafter tie raised

Additional purlin as required

Insulating board

C

Quilted insulating material

Skirting

fig 26

fig 25

Existing Joists

Strengtheners

Noggings

53

permit greater light entry than building a dormer window, Fig.28, which, because of corners encountered, will throw parts of the new room into shadow. On the other hand, a dormer looks more imposing from the outside.

Making your own roof light with teak or western red cedar is an extremely complicated job as it will have to keep out rain when closed. So it may be cheaper in the end to buy a prefabricated one obtainable in aluminium alloy, galvanized steel or zinc with full instructions for fitting.

When removing the necessary roofing tiles, support the tops of those that have to be cut with strips of wood to compensate for loss of tilt. Cross-noggings may be nailed with galvanized nails, and for other parts use brass screws so that you have no trouble with rust. The glass pane is secured with mastic and clips. Mastic should also be 'buttered' on the face of all joins. Add narrow strips of bituminous felt at exterior joins of movable parts. Fix a stay at the bottom of the window for ease of manipulation.

**Structural alterations**   A typical design of high-pitched roof is shown in Fig.26A, though it will vary according to the type of house and the period in which it was built. Your roof may not include all the members shown. Diagonal struts will possibly take the place of queen posts, but these and the king posts won't *necessarily* present much obstruction. The rafter ties may be too low and need cutting shorter and replacing higher up as is shown in **A** and **B** to make the statutory ceiling height possible. Work on one tie at a time or the roof may bulge.

Water cisterns may need repositioning to come behind the partition walls of the new room. In any case, examine them to ensure they're sound because, once the room is lined, you won't want to pull the walls about to replace them. At the same time see there are no loose tiles or perished flaunching (the join at base of chimney pots). Examine the rafters for woodworm and treat as described in chapter 10.

**Insulation and wiring**   Insulate the roof with quilted material nailed on to the rafters or the room will be uncomfortably hot or icy cold.

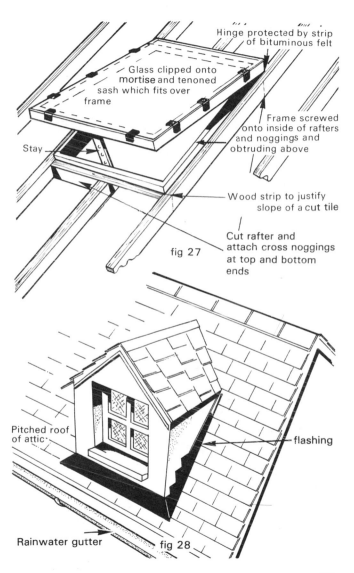

Hinge protected by strip of bituminous felt

Glass clipped onto **mortise** and tenoned sash which fits over frame

Frame screwed onto inside of rafters and noggings and obtruding above

Stay

Wood strip to justify slope of a cut tile

Cut rafter and attach cross noggings at top and bottom ends

fig 27

Pitched roof of attic

flashing

Rainwater gutter

fig 28

55

Have the room wired for lighting and heating and then raise 50×50mm (2×2in) studs from floor to rafters as is shown in Fig.20, page 45. Nail 20×30mm (¾×1¼in) battens to the exposed bricks of the gable and line the whole lot, horizontal ceiling, sloping ceiling and walls, with insulating board. You will have to cut the edges of the board extremely true; and the quickest way is to attend to the ceiling first, leaving a slight overlap. Butt the sloping ceiling pieces up to that, also overlapping at the bottom side; then do the walls, butting on to the sloping parts. There's no need to be too particular with the bottoms of the vertical wall pieces because the skirting-board will take up any irregularities.

An alternative to insulating board is the use of slabs of compressed straw, known as Stramit, which would give even better insulation than the board.

**Floor**   Whether you lay flooring before or after securing wall and ceiling linings will depend on the arrangement of your attic space. An advantage of seeing to the floor first is that it may, if desired, extend under the eaves space behind the walls for storage purposes. Another advantage of lining walls last is that pins use to secure the panels won't be loosened by vibration caused through nailing on floorboards.

Tongued-and-grooved flooring presents few problems until you come to the last length which has to be cut accurately to width and the tongue sawn off to get the piece into position. This board with a method of secret nailing is shown on page 26.

A method of getting square or plain-edged boards to fit tightly is shown in Fig.29. Nail on the first board permanently; then squeeze up succeeding boards by rough-nailing battens to strategic joists and hammering wedges in between. The battens can be moved along as you go.

When nailing the floor, watch the ceiling below because, here again, vibration may result in the loosening of plaster. If there is any doubt it might be wiser though more time-consuming to use screws instead of nails, counter-sinking them of course.

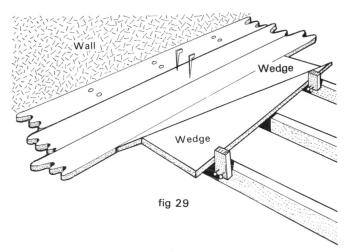

Wall

Wedge

Wedge

fig 29

**Ceiling and walls**  You will have lined the top horizontal part of the ceiling first with slighter wider panels than are required. Then butted on sloping panels which are longer at the bottom and lastly the wall panels. If small gaps show between joins, fill with a mastic compound which will give with expansion and contraction and not drop out; or you can use cover strips. Hide the gap between bottom of wall panels and flooring with a skirting-board the most convenient form being 40mm (1½in) quadrant moulding, Fig.22, page 48. Nail to floorboards only not, as many do, alternately to floor and wall studs. They will then give with structural movement and won't tear the wood.

# TABLE 5

**Minimum joist strength**

| Width and thickness | | Distance apart | | Maximum span | |
|---|---|---|---|---|---|
| Metric mm | Imp. in | Metric mm | Imp. in | Metric m. | Imp. ft/in |
| 100 × 50 | 4 × 2 | 400 | 16 | 1.93 | 6/4 |
| | | 460 | 18 | 1.75 | 5/9 |
| | | 530 | 21 | 1.52 | 5 |
| 125 × 50 | 5 × 2 | 400 | 16 | 2.59 | 8/6 |
| | | 460 | 18 | 2.49 | 8/2 |
| | | 530 | 21 | 2.31 | 7/7 |
| 150 × 50 | 6 × 2 | 400 | 16 | 3.12 | 10/3 |
| | | 460 | 18 | 3.00 | 9/10 |
| | | 530 | 21 | 2.82 | 9/3 |
| 200 × 50 | 8 × 2 | 400 | 16 | 4.24 | 13/11 |
| | | 460 | 18 | 4.04 | 13/3 |
| | | 530 | 21 | 3.84 | 12/7 |
| 225 × 50 | 9 × 2 | 400 | 16 | 4.75 | 15/7 |
| | | 460 | 18 | 4.55 | 14/11 |
| | | 530 | 21 | 4.27 | 14 |

# TABLE 6

**Floorboards**

| Type | Thickness | | Max. distance between joists | |
|---|---|---|---|---|
| | Metric mm | Imp. in | Metric mm | Imp. in |
| Tongued-and-grooved | 19 | 3/4 | 405 | 16 |
| | 22 | 7/8 | 460 | 18 |
| | 25 | 1 | 530 | 21 |
| Plain or square edged | 22 | 7/8 | 405 | 16 |
| | 25 | 1 | 460 | 18 |

# 5. KITCHENS AND BATHROOMS

Food often tastes at its best in an old farmhouse kitchen where the cooking is carried out in the same room as that in which it is eaten. It can then be served straight on to plates without having to keep it warm.

Where space is at a premium there's a reversion to this form of home planning, sometimes incorporating a partition built between cooking and eating areas.

## Kitchen planning

Kitchens vary so much in size and shape that no one plan will cover every eventuality; but careful consideration should be afforded to arrangement with due regard to the miles walked in the course of a month between stove, fridge and sink! Take a critical look at your kitchen and try to halve the walking distance in preparing a meal.

A side-hung door could be superseded by a sliding one to save space and remember that doors can, of course, be hinged on the right instead of the left.

The ideal kitchen contains a double sink, one for soapless detergent solution and the other for rinsing. Important because detergent left behind in cups can impart an unpleasant taste to delicate flavours. There should be two draining boards, one for dirty dishes and the other for washed dishes. Wherever possible convert the tops of cupboards and drawers into working tops, you can't have too many of them. A top adjoining the cooking stove is particularly useful. Consider adding a folding flap which needs lifting only occasionally when getting at lesser used articles. If there is room leave space under the right draining board so that work can be done seated at the sink. A folding table and stackable chairs can save space.

There should be ample electric sockets, at least four, to plug in electric kettle, mixers and so on. It's exasperating to keep on unplugging and plugging where there are only one or two sockets and using adaptors can be unsafe.

## Bathroom

If you have time to make bathing a ritual and the money to spend you can buy circular baths with gold taps, baths with head and arm rests, double baths and sunken baths. A long cry from the hip bath and the tin tub which was hung on a nail on the wall outside until Saturday night when it was brought in and stood in front of the kitchen range while water was boiling in the copper! Most of us are quite contented with the conventional shape of bath with, perhaps the luxury of a handrail to lever us up and a non-slip bottom. Modern baths are either glazed steel or glass fibre and the former, with constant use by the usual size of family, will last 16 to 20 years without reglazing by professionals *in situ* and much longer if you don't employ abrasive powders for cleaning.

**Badly neglected baths**  If your bath has started to change colour, treat the patches with one of the excellent bath-stain removers on the market. Wipe chromium taps underneath as well as on top or a lime deposit will accumulate.

A bath that has become too worn for the cleaning methods given above is better replaced with a new one. This will interfere with existing plumbing and wall decorations. Some companies will, however, reglaze a bath *in situ* without such inconveniences and at much less cost.

Doing the job yourself is neck-aching work and plenty of ventilation will have to be provided to disperse paint fumes entrapped within the well of the bath. The best of hand-applied bath enamels won't have the wearing properties of the original glaze. The original surface will have to be thoroughly cleaned with detergent solution and wirewool, swilled down and left to dry. Tie empty jam jars under taps in case a drip of water forms. Place a lintless cloth over the near edge of the bath on which you can rest your arm. Start in the middle of the far edge and work to right and left and downwards. Then attend to the ends and bottom and finally the near side. No harsh abrasive powders can be used for subsequent cleaning and the cold tap turned on first when running a bath to allow the difference in coefficients of expansion to catch up gradually with each other. Don't use the bath or allow steam to collect in the room for four or five days after painting to allow the enamel to harden.

## Showers

A shower takes about two-thirds less hot water than a bath, so saving fuel, and it takes about half the time to cleanse the body, a consideration for busy people.

A cabinet containing a shower and nothing else serves as a useful second bathroom but, for economy's sake, it should be positioned near the water supply. If there's no spare space for a separate shower, fix it at the tap end of the bath tub, with a rail overhead on to which impervious curtain material can be hung. When using the shower, tuck the bottom of the curtain inside the bath or the floor will become flooded.

You may want to install the shower yourself instead of employing a plumber. Buy it in kit form with detailed installation instructions which should be followed meticulously.

## Refurbishing tiled walls

Adequate illustrated instructions for retiling walls above baths and washbasins are given by tile manufacturers and there is no need to repeat them. A gap between bath or basin and wall can be sealed by self-adhesive strips sold for the purpose.

Tiles on old walls have generally been mortared on and their removal will result in damage to underlying plaster. If they are in a bad state, clean them thoroughly, removing any detergent solution used, and paint them with two thin finishing coats of an alkyd resin paint or a polyurethane paint which is harder. Don't use a primer which is too oily or an undercoat which is too highly pigmented to adhere properly.

An alternative, which is more expensive, is to stick self-adhesive film, cut to size, on top. This can be obtained from do-it-yourself shops either plain or in attractive designs.

Dirty grouting (joins between tiles) can be cleaned with a stiff brush or ink eraser and kept that way for a long period by touching in with a transparent silicone water-proofing solution which repels dirt-laden moisture.

# 6.DOORS,WINDOWS AND ROOM TRIM

## Doors

Timber swells with moisture and shrinks on drying. So if a door starts sticking for the first time in years it'll probably be due to your having a prolonged holiday during wet weather when there was no interior heating.

Don't plane off the opening edge until you've examined the hinges. Screws may have become loose and require tightening to pull the hanging edge in. If there's still a serious overlap and screws keep turning without tightening, use larger screws or plug the holes and rescrew. When this doesn't cure the fault, and after the door is perfectly dry, remove from its hinges and chisel out a very little more of the rebate holding the hinge flange. You will have to do this cautiously and by trial and error or you will be faced with the opposite trouble, a wide gap at the opening edge. Only as a last resort use a plane.

A wide gap at the opening edge, which often happens with a new house when central heating has been installed, may necessitate padding out of the rebate with thin card to bring the *opening* edge nearer the jamb.

If, when buying a new door, you cannot find one which fits the existing doorcase precisely, buy one slightly over-size, get a colleague to hold it tightly against the outside of the doorcase and trace round with pencil. Saw to this mark and then plane to allow 1.5mm ($\frac{1}{16}$in) tolerance, leaving a slightly wider gap at the bottom to prevent fouling the floor. When cutting, make sure you don't interfere too much with mortise-and-tenon joints.

**Twisting door** Factory produced doors often twist fairly quickly. With an outside door this can be corrected by fixing a barrel bolt where the twist is widest. If an inside door, there's nothing for it but to remove the door stop, the jutting-out piece on to which the door closes, plane its edge to shape with a spokeshave and refix nearer. Don't make it such a tight fit as to cause 'set-off' of coats of paint when the door is shut.

**Flush doors**   Old-fashioned panel doors will have been made by a craftsman while the house was being built. These doors have a beauty of their own which it is sacrilege to hide. If the panels are badly cracked, however, or there are too many indentations which it would be hopeless to stop up, then you can pin on fibreboard sheeting (page 18) to hide the damage. Condition it with water scrubbed on the back, leave for about 48 hours and cut to size. The extra thickness added to the door will obviously foul the door stop which will have to be moved out a little. If you don't want to go to this trouble, cut the fibreboard about 40mm (1½in) less than the width of the door and centre it with the same margin at the top. Leave a wider margin of old door at the bottom – say about 100mm (4in) – because the centre of sight isn't plumb in the middle of anything; it's always a little way up. Bull-nose to round the edges of the cut fibreboard with file and glasspaper. Make good the gaps between panels and sheathing with pieces of wood of the right thickness screwed to the panels, as is shown in Fig.30.

**Cupboard doors**   Alcoves in modern houses are seldom if ever built to a true rectangle. Older houses may be worse owing to subsidence. Suppose you wish to enclose such a recess with a door, build the doorcase or frame first with battens which, when screwed into plugged holes in the masonry, will bend with structural irregularities.
    This leaves the problem of cutting the shape of the door with the same irregularities, which would mean extremely accurate measurements. Certainly gaps between doorcase and wall can be padded out with cellulose stopper to keep the battens straight, but even then the corners may not be rectangular. One way out of the difficulty is to cut the door oversize so that it slightly overlaps sides, top and bottom edges. This is called a lay-on door, Fig.31A.

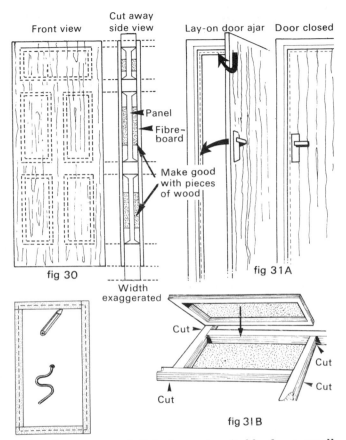

**Front view**

**Cut away side view**

Panel

Fibreboard

Make good with pieces of wood

Width exaggerated

fig 30

**Lay-on door ajar** **Door closed**

fig 31A

Cut

Cut

Cut

Cut

fig 31B

Another way, and this is most suitable for a small opening of, say, a high-reach cupboard, is to place a piece of 3.2mm (⅛in) hardboard, smooth side out, behind the doorcase. Hold it there by the best means possible, either with assistance or by boring a small hole in the centre, passing knotted string through and pulling, and mark round with a pencil. The hole can be camouflaged later with cellulose stopper, Cut round the pencil mark as is shown in Fig.31B.

Lay another piece of oversize board, rough side up, flat on the floor. Lay the cut piece on top, this time rough side down, trace round with a pencil and cut. You will now have two pieces of exact shape and dimensions. Coat the edges of the bottom piece with wood adhesive and stick on lengths of batten all round to line up with the edges. Turn it over gently so that the battens don't move and further secure with lost-head panel pins at intervals of about 75mm (3in), 5mm (³⁄₁₆in) from the edges. Turn the whole lot over once again and glue and pin on the second piece of hardboard, rough side down. A cross brace may be needed if the door is extra wide.

This door will now fit so precisely that it will neither open nor close without tugging. So give a few passes with a plane all round to give a tolerance of 1.5mm (¹⁄₁₆in). Before painting the door, seal in porosity with a well-thinned coat of emulsion. No further priming will be needed.

**Sliding and folding doors**   Over 1m² (10sq.ft) of floor area is required to open a side-hinged door to its fullest extent. A folding door, made on the principle of an accordian, will take ⅕ of this space and a sliding door takes no space at all. Two points to bear in mind before deciding on one of these to save space in a small dwelling: there must be no obstructions to prevent the door from opening to its fullest extent; and if you use an existing doorcase it will have to be cut down at one side and part of the skirting-board removed to give freedom of movement. Fittings for such doors are sold in kit form. To prevent draughts, choose the type designed to pull the door in tightly when closed.

# Picture rails

Don't remove picture rails without due thought. They visually reduce the height of a high ceiling because the eye tends to follow them through to right and left. Another reason for not taking off these rails is that the frieze above is likely to be the first part of a wall to show cracks. At

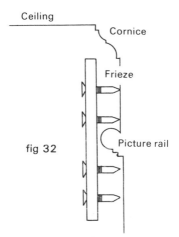

Ceiling

Cornice

Frieze

fig 32

Picture rail

some time in the past it may have been replastered and the level may not be the same as that underneath, leaving you with an unsightly bulge. Test this by knocking four nails into a short, perfectly straight batten so that the points protrude precisely at the same distance. Offer this to the wall vertically so that two nails come below the rail and two above. Any gaps between nail points and wall will show there is unevenness, Fig.32.

If you *must* discard a picture rail, locate slight depressions in the surface which will indicate where it has been nailed on. If the nail depressions have been stopped up as they should have been, pass a powerful magnet over and it'll be attracted by the metal.

Cut close up to the nail heads with a tenon saw and the middles will fall out or, if stuck with old paint, lever off with a blunt chisel. Now chisel off the pieces left behind by splitting them in the direction of the grain of the wood until the nail is exposed. Extract with a claw hammer and, if it breaks off, punch it right in. It remains to stop up holes and unevenness with cellulose stopper. As you'll be faced with old plaster and new patches whose absorbencies may differ it is safest to line the walls before decorating.

# Windows

Through frequent opening and closing, mortise-and-tenon joints of casement window frames sometimes become loose. Knock them home with a wooden mallet, not a hammer or cracking of the glass may result; secure with brass screws to avoid rusting. Stop up screw-head depressions with cellulose stopper and sand level.

Casement windows that won't readily open and close result from neglect to keep paintwork in good condition, allowing moisture to enter and swell the wood frame. The remedy is to wait for dry weather, secure loose joints as indicated above, putty up cracks and repaint. Another cause is a fatty edge of old paint on a bottom rail. Scrape off with a shave hook before repainting and use only a thin coat on this vital part.

The sticking of sliding sash windows is generally the result of an accumulation of old paint between stiles and corresponding beads. Remove the staff beads, take out the lower sash and scrape both sash and sides of beads. Remove parting bead, take out the upper sash and scrape. If the upper sash rattles in a high wind, renew the parting bead with a thicker one. This should also take care of rattle in the lower sash. If not, nail the staff bead a little closer. New paint on the lower sash can run down to form a fatty edge at the bottom. Even if this accumulation may be only 1mm (1/16in) or less it will prevent the meeting rails from lining up when the window is closed with the result that the window catch fails to engage. This also requires scraping.

It is wise to open and close windows twice a day for about a week to stop new paint from bridging over joins before it has hardened.

A questionable improvement to the old-fashioned sliding sash which works with hidden compensating weights is a side-sprung cord where no weights are needed. Its adequacy is a matter for opinion because, if the frame swells, it will hug the spring so closely that opening can be done only with brute force. You can, however, smear the side runners with graphite; and penetrating oil squeezed in from the top will give a similar result, though you'll

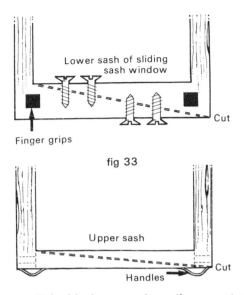

Lower sash of sliding sash window

Finger grips

Cut

fig 33

Upper sash

Cut

Handles

have to wipe off the black mess when oil runs out at the bottom.

Suppose you wish to install a new aluminium or steel-framed window and find it clashes with the remaining wooden ones, clean with white spirit and *fine* wire wool or a coarse cloth wetted with white spirit (turpentine substitute) and apply a coat of zinc chromate primer for aluminium, and calcium plumbate primer for new zinc galvanizing before repainting.

An old wooden window sash may be sound except for the bottom rail which is prone to premature rotting through rain running down the pane, you can replace it by the method shown in Fig.33. Cut a new length of rebated sash moulding diagonally and with tenons to fit the old mortises. Rub the diagonal join with mastic compound to make it waterproof. Push each tenon into the corresponding mortise and screw the separated lengths together with brass screws and stop up level. Fit handles at both ends so that, when opening and closing, the strain is taken up by the stiles.

**Leaded lights**  The fashion at the turn of the century was to have leaded windows to front door, hall and staircase, with different shapes and colours of glass; in short, stained glass windows.

If one of the panes breaks, cut open the intersecting joins with a sharp knife, open up one side of the lead strip and take out the broken pieces. By trial and error, cut two cardboard templates to shape and take one to a reputable glass merchant with a piece of the broken glass to indicate weight and colour. As he will have to send it away to a craftsman specialist, some weeks may elapse before you get delivery of the new glass; so pop the second template in the gap to prevent ingress of rain. On delivery of the new piece try it out to make sure it fits. A slight outward bulge can be corrected with a carborundum stick or carborundum paper wrapped round a block of wood. Now smear the edges with mastic compound and insert permanently in the gap. Press the opened lead strip back into position carefully, making sure the cut-lead joins meet.

This will be quite an expensive job so in parts not readily noticed, scribe a piece of plain glass to the size of the template and snip round the curved edges with pliers, little by little. Give it a coat of alkyd resin paint which, if thin enough, will be translucent. Paint only the inside.

You can buy lead in ready-made strips for sticking on to a plain glass pane and, being malleable, they can be bent to various designs. You can also get self-adhesive translucent vinyl in various coloured designs to stick over a plain glass window, after cleaning thoroughly.

**Frosted glass**  Glazing is carried out with the rough or reeded side inwards, leaving the plain side, which will get dirty quicker, towards the outside. If you want to achieve a frosted appearance on plain glass in sound condition, clean it, rub over with methylated spirit and give a thin finishing coat (no primer or undercoat) of alkyd resin paint. While the coating is still wet, dab it with a non-fluffy cloth to raise the surface and destroy the high gloss. Frosted self-adhesive vinyl can also be used to achieve a similar effect.

# 7. CEILINGS, FLOORS AND STAIRS

The low ceiling of a modern house can be made to appear higher by decorating it in white or in a very light pastel colour containing a little blue, this being a receding tone. The high ceiling of an old house can be brought down with a designed paper, the predominant colour of which is a lighter shade than that of the floor covering.

**Suspended ceiling** A ceiling that is too high wastes heat. Fit a suspended ceiling beneath in the way shown in Fig.34. Measurements will have to be amended to suit the size of the room; but for an average sized room fix 50×25mm (2×1in) wood wallplates to a solid wall with masonry nails. If the walls are hollow, locate the studs by one of the methods given on page 35 and use ordinary, non-ferrous wood screws. Make sure the plates are horizontal by using the edge of a straight board with a spirit level on top. Mark with a pencil all round the room and where the line begins and ends should meet. Check the straightness of the board by 'sighting' it as on page 17 which shows how to prove a door that may be twisted.

T-half join plates on opposing walls with 50×50mm (2×2in) battens of length equal to the span of the room splicing them if necessary to achieve the length. Centres (distances between T-joints) will be determined by the width of the plasterboard sheathing. If they are not more than 400mm (16in) apart, there will be little danger of sagging. Several battens may come within the width of the plasterboard but one *must* come immediately above a join. Add cross-noggings where the ends of the sheathing meet, Fig. 34. The joins of the board must be staggered.

If you prefer, you can pass the sheathing up between the battens and lay them loosely on top of this framework,

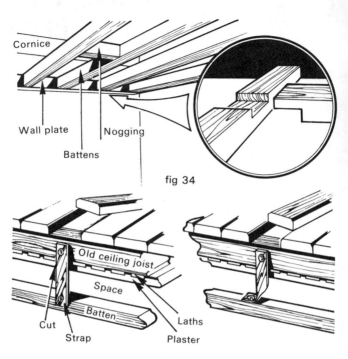

Cornice

Wall plate

Battens

Nogging

fig 34

Old ceiling joist

Space

Batten

Cut

Strap

Laths

Plaster

fig 35

leaving the battens exposed and staining and varnishing them. The last sheet laid will have to be extremely accurately cut and require some ingenuity to get it into position. Alternatively, the sheeting can be pinned on underneath. Where cross battens tend to sag in the middle, strap them to the joists above with thin mild steel bars, twisting the ends so that they won't show. There will be no need to twist the straps for a plain surfaced suspended ceiling as they will be hidden. No need to remove the old plaster, slots to take the straps can be cut out using a chisel, Fig.35.

Leave about 3mm (⅛in) between each sheet to allow for movement and scrim and plaster the gaps. A more elegant way would be to stick or pin on plastic or wooden cover strips; and these can be arranged to form a pleasing pattern even where they are not required to hide a gap.

**Cracks** Cracks in a ceiling can be disguised with a plastic textured paint after the wider cracks have been stopped with cellulose stopper. Use a trowel to achieve an irregular pattern, a brush to produce whorls, a paint roller covered with polythene sheeting to simulate the raised grain of sawn timber and, for a bumpy effect, even out the paint with a plasterer's float and then pull it smartly away. When dry, sharp protuberances may be smoothed off lightly with abrasive paper wrapped round a block of wood of convenient handling size. A further variety of relief patterns and showing how to achieve them are given in manufacturers' instructional literature. Some of these products are self-coloured and others require painting.

Walls as well as ceilings may be coated with textured paints though they will hold dust which has to be removed with a soft banister brush or vacuum cleaner. Washing them isn't easy and can be done only with a brush and soapless detergent, removing all traces of detergent afterwards with plain water.

**Beamed ceilings** To achieve a 'cottagey' effect on ceilings of old property, you can buy extremely faithful imitations in light-weight plastic from do-it-yourself shops. These can be stuck on to the existing ceiling or screwed through the plaster to joists above. Areas in between can be painted in white emulsion.

If only one or two beams are required and you wish them to jut down from the ceiling by several inches, go to a demolition contractor or see the foreman supervising an ancient cottage being pulled down. Or you can buy new timber and 'distress' it by standing it outside the backdoor and every time you go in and out, give it a hearty swipe with a heavy dog chain. Using an axe or adze doesn't give a sufficiently rough effect and looks artificial. Such a beam will be weighty. If you have no help, wedge it in position against the ceiling with stout posts while you counterbore holes to take screws for entry into the joists above.

Excessively long timbers may have to be supported in holes in the wall at each side.

# Floors

Staining and sealing floorboards with polyurethane isn't always all that satisfactory. No coating will withstand the constant scuffing of feet and an unsealed surface will need frequent polishing. Slip mats will have to be placed at points of most foot traffic; doors, windows and fireplaces, and polish should *not* be applied under these or they may slide and cause accidents. Before laying any kind of floor covering check that the floorboards are firm and level. Punch in all protruding nail heads. You may be able to plane the edges of warped floorboards or use a sanding machine which can be hired from a builders' hire service. With extremely bad floors, lay fibreboard on top, loosely, rough side uppermost.

**Squeaking floorboards** A squeak in the floorboard is caused through the edges of two boards rubbing against each other. Punch the nails farther in or add more nails driven askew. Where old boards have become tatty through frequent removal, use countersunk wood screws. Insert strips of wood glued at both sides between badly shrunken floorboards and plane level when dry. For narrow gaps poke in nylon string and stop over to the right height with cellulose filler. Very narrow gaps will need knifed-in filler only.

**Relaying a floor** Tongued-and-grooved boards are more expensive than those that are square or plain edged and are more difficult to lift if occasion arises; but they help to prevent dust rising from underneath and have less tendency to warp at the edges. To ensure a tight fit, nail the first plank down permanently at one side of the room, grooved side out. Rough-nail two short battens to a convenient joist and hammer in triangular wedges before nailing succeeding boards as is shown in Fig.29. Move batten along as you go. On approaching the opposite side of the room, the wall will act as a support for the wedges. Saw off the tongue of the last board for ease of insertion.

**Concrete floor**   It may not be possible to improve ventilation under suspended ground flooring, with the resulting danger of an outbreak of dry rot. That being the case, rip up boards and joists and, if the subfloor has not already been concreted, tamp down hardcore. Over this shovel about 100mm (4in) of concrete (say, 1 of cement and 4 of sand) and finish off by placing a spirit level on the top edge of a long straight board, jogging it up and down to compact the mass. Two people will be required for this, one at each end of the board. Then lay a 500 grade polythene dampproof membrane and bring the edges up at the sides to join up with the wall damp-proof course (d.p.c.). Now screed over the top with more mortar to a depth of some 40mm (1½in). Wood or composition tiles may be stuck on top.

**Vinyl**   This has largely taken the place of linoleum and shrinks whereas linoleum expands; that is why the latter has to be trimmed round the edges a few weeks after being laid. In shrinking, vinyl tends to curl at the edges unless it is stuck down to a perfectly level floor. As these materials are impervious make sure airbricks function properly or you could get an outbreak of dry rot.
   Vinyl and cork can be laid virtually to any floor, concrete, composition or wood, provided it is dry and expected to remain dry. Bitumen spread over a damp floor is of no earthly use; there must be a damp-proof membrane *underneath*. The use of an adhesive may not be advisable over surfaces other than timber or hardboard. Consult the manager of the shop where you buy the vinyl. The sheeting is obtainable with its own resilient backing or, if the pattern of your choice has no backing, underlay it with grey paper felt which can be bought at the same time.

**Carpets**   Needless to say, if you carpet over an uneven floor the boards will show through in humps and there will be more wear. Some carpets come with their own backing. Rubber-backed carpets can cause problems. If a liquid is spilt and soaks through, the rubber will stick to the floor so that, when you want to lift the covering, patches of rubber are left behind and will need scraping off. This will not only weaken the pile but destroy the effectiveness of the underlay.

If you are having a separate underlay, place sheets of newspaper underneath for additional protection. If you don't, in the case of an old square or plain-boarded floor showing gaps, dust will rise from the subfloor and show as black ridges on the face of the carpet.

A professional with the right tools will lay a wall-to-wall fitted carpet in no time. Doing it yourself isn't as easy as it sounds and needs grippers around the perimeter of the room. Grippers are strips of wood or metal with spikes arranged at an angle pointing towards the wall.

Using a sharp knife, cut round door architraves as is shown on page 78. For a bay window shape roughly oversize and nick down corners and cut. Other room irregularities can be treated similarly. Transfer width measurement of one side of an abutting wall to the carpet with chalk with about 25mm (1in) overlap. Cut down at this mark and trim at juncture of wall and floor. Lay the carpet loosely and, kneeling in the middle, push it away from you as tightly as you can, using a short plank of wood. Secure temporarily over the gripper spikes and leave for a few months to allow for stretching. Then repeat the process, this time pressing it permanently over the grippers. Large tacks cost less than grippers but aren't so easy to manipulate when taking up after stretching.

Before decorating a room that has a fitted carpet, bend over the parts that cover bays and recesses to form a rectangle. Then fold corners diagonally towards opposing corners so that they meet in the centre of the room. This will form a new smaller rectangle. Fold the corners again in the same way until you get a neat heap in the centre of the room where it can be covered with a sheet of polythene for protection. When the time comes to unfold it, the carpet will fall back in the right position – which cannot be achieved by rolling it.

**Carpet Squares**  These may be bought in a variety of

colours or all in one colour. Some need adhesive, some are self-adhesive and others are laid loosely on the floor without kicking up at the edges. The loosely laid squares are excellent for evening out wear because they can be changed round as required.

**Cork**  Cork is soft to the tread and, to a degree, reduces sound transference. On the other hand, grit tends to tread in and is almost impossible to remove. To a large extent this can be minimised by sealing the surface with a sealer. Care should be taken when selecting this as some shouldn't be used in a steamy atmosphere as they tend to 'bloom' when subjected to an excess of moisture. Again, the floor must be perfectly level before laying the cork.

**Tiles**  Whatever kind of tiles you decide to invest in, vinyl, cork, or composition, the floor on to which they are stuck must be perfectly clean and perfectly level. The adhesive to be used will be stated in the manufacturer's sales literature.

Mark the centre of the widest part of the room and also of the longest and draw chalk marks to cross each other at right-angles. Work on one quarter at a time, spreading the adhesive on the floor over an area of about $1m^2$ (square yard) and, starting at the centre, lay the first tile to line up with your intersecting chalk marks. Continue until the whole of this quarter is completed. Then proceed with the next quarter, and so on, working towards the door, Fig.36.

Refer to Fig.37 when you reach near the side of the room. Lay one tile, A, loosely and another, B, to overlap it and touch the skirting-board. Scribe tile A at the overlap and cut. Now reverse the positions of A and B and stick them down.

To make a close fit round an awkward protuberance say, an architrave, use a forma tool which comprises a number of steel needles imprisoned in a clamp. Push the forma against the protuberance, screw up the clamp and transfer the shape to the tile. Scribe round the design and snip off unwanted pieces with pincers, Fig.38.

If you have no forma, use compasses as is shown in Fig.39. The compasses you have may not open wide

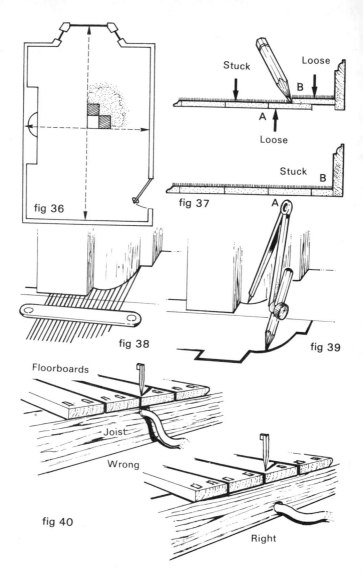

Stuck

Loose

B

A

Loose

fig 37

Stuck

B

A

fig 36

fig 38

fig 39

Floorboards

Joist

Wrong

Right

fig 40

enough. In that case, make a larger pair from two narrow pieces of wood bolted at one end to form a hinge. A similar procedure can be followed with all-over linoleum and vinyl sheeting.

**Wood blocks** Parquet flooring can be obtained in various thicknesses and laid in a variety of attractive designs. As the manufacturer will give full instructions for laying there's no need to repeat them.

As there is a certain amount of surface wear, lay slip mats at strategic intervals, doors, windows and fireplaces, and don't polish underneath in case they slide and cause an accident.

A word of warning; anything that is stuck down will be more or less permanent. Loosely laid material is preferable so that one can easily get to underfloor service pipes, cables and so on.

By the way, if you're laying an electric cable under a floor don't make a groove in the top of a joist as most electricians do. Bore a hole a little way down so that, if a nail has to be driven into a loose floorboard, the cable won't be punctured, Fig.40.

# Stairs

Open-plan stairs are shown in Fig.41. These are suitable only for dwellings on two floors because they form a funnel in the event of fire. Anything higher will need risers as well as treads, Fig. 42, and should have fireproof sheathing attached underneath. This sheathing is a nuisance if you want to effect any repairs caused by, say, blocks becoming unstuck when glue has cracked through central heating.

Steep stairs, where the height of the risers is the same as the width of the treads, are not only dangerous, they're uncomfortable to climb. The more usual riser is some 180mm (7in) and tread 230mm (9in). The best, which can only be seen in large houses affording sufficient space, have 150mm (6in) risers and 290mm (11½in) treads. They allow the whole foot to step on something firm and are often found in old people's homes. In addition to safety and

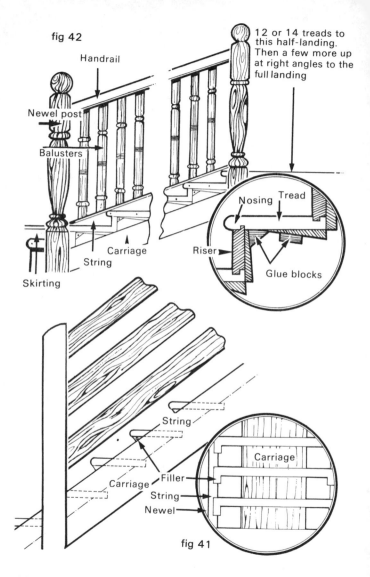

fig 42

Handrail

Newel post

Balusters

Carriage

String

Skirting

12 or 14 treads to this half-landing. Then a few more up at right angles to the full landing

Nosing    Tread

Riser

Glue blocks

String

Carriage

Filler

Carriage

String

Newel

fig 41

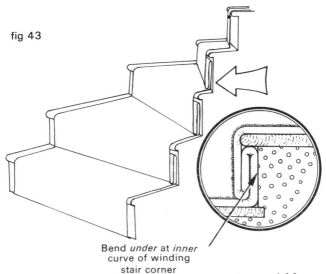

fig 43

Bend *under* at *inner*
curve of winding
stair corner

comfort they don't wear a stair carpet out so quickly as they entail less scuffing of feet.

**Squeaking stairs** Squeaking is caused by the rubbing together of loose treads and risers. If you don't want to remove the under-sheathing to replace the retaining blocks you can bring the loose parts close together with countersunk screws. Temporary relief can be given by injecting french chalk into the joints with a rubber puff.

**Laying a stair carpet** Mark the width of the carpet in the centre of the treads with chalk and screw in grippers to come within the confines of these marks.

Start at the bottom and work up, stretching the carpet and hammering over the spikes of the grippers with a piece of plywood or hardboard. Leave about 400mm or 16in of carpet at the bottom so that, at spring-cleaning time, you can shift the carpet up to even out wear. Turn the spare piece under to act as an underfelt for the bottom tread. All other treads should have pieces of underlay cut to fit over the nosing. Don't turn the carpet the other way round as the pile will run in the wrong direction, resulting in undue wear.

With a square half landing, the carpet will naturally have to be cut at this point. If the stair winds there is no need to cut. Just stretch the long edge, the one nearest the wall, tuck the overlap nearest the balusters underneath at each riser and tack down. Make sure the overlap contacts the riser upwards and *underneath* or dust will collect, Fig.43.

**Balusters** Newel posts and balusters support the handrail. In old houses there would be two to each tread, often highly ornate and difficult to dust. If they become loose you will have to examine the way they are fixed. Maybe they are attached to the stringer or inlet into the treads. With the former, rescrewing may be the answer. In the latter case, a wobble can often be corrected by hammering thin glued wedges into any gaps, but make sure they remain upright with a vertical spirit level.

Cleaning balusters is a time-consuming process, all very well in the days of cheap domestic labour. These days people would perhaps prefer the ranch type. Planks should be about 120×40mm (4¾×1½in) and mortised-and-tenoned into the newel posts. A simpler way of erection would be to screw them to the outsides of the newels, Fig.41.

Handrails are generally of varnished and polished hardwood, needing only an occasional wipe down and revarnishing from time to time. Make sure old varnish is well sanded down or removed with a non-caustic paint remover before applying new varnish.

# 8.FIREPLACES AND CHIMNEYS

The latter part of the 20th century will be remembered as a period of houses without fireplaces or chimneys, homes without souls! The crackling fire may be coming back into its own so if you have a fireplace in keeping with the period of your house don't rush to take it out.

**Removing a fireplace** If, however, the original has been replaced with an ugly modern surround and you *must* take it out, it's not very difficult. There will be a lot of lime and sooty mess flying round so remove all furniture, take up the carpet and get the chimney swept.

Most surrounds are fastened to the wall at the sides by lugs that can be levered out. If concealed in plaster, chip some away and you will be able to get at them. Enlist the help of a colleague to support the weight or the whole contraption will fall on you and it will be very heavy. Seal up the opening with plasterboard, boring a few holes near the bottom for adequate ventilation. Position the holes a few inches up or debris and remaining soot could fall behind and foul them. If the chimney isn't ventilated by these holes, condensation could form inside and force soot left behind in the chimney to bleed through and ruin the decorations. If this has already happened, seal over the defect with pitch paper before redecorating. Fit a cowl over the top of the chimney to keep rain out and, for aesthetic considerations, please don't have the chimney dismantled.

When an extremely jagged hole is left in the chimney breast after removal of a fireplace, plug sound parts of the wall and secure plasterboard with brass screws so that it comes slightly inside surrounding wall area. Then plaster over the top to achieve an even surface.

To fit a new fire surround, rebuild any brickwork

necessary to less than the dimensions of the surround and secure to the side walls through side lugs which are provided. If further tiles are needed buy the fire-resisting type. Often these may be obtained from a demolition contractor's yard.

**Smoky chimneys**  Air that has been heated by an open fire rises with fumes and goes up the chimney – but only if more air enters the room to take its place. When a room is hermetically sealed and you don't allow for at least a little ventilation, the fire will go out and lack of oxygen leads to headaches.

With hollow floors, a vent in the flooring at both sides will provide fresh air. Fittings are made to fit these holes with valves allowing air to enter but not get out. Or you can have a fire fed by underfloor draught. It'll be sucked in through outside airbricks, not only providing the oxygen needed to keep the fire alight but helping to keep the underpart ventilated, so minimising the danger of dry rot.

When a fire hasn't been lit for some time, the chimney lining gets cold. Light the first fire and warm air will rise up the chimney, cool quickly and drop – bringing smoke with it into the room. All you can do in this case is to experiment with slightly opened and closed doors to create a draught until the chimney warms up. This fault occurs mostly with chimneys built on an outside wall exposed to wind and rain.

If bricks at the top of a chimney are at all porous, rain on evaporating will chill the whole stack. When this occurs, replace pointing and give two applications of a silicone waterproofing solution. When aloft and examining the stack see that flaunching and flashing are sound and also oversailing course, whose object is to throw rain clear, Fig. 44.

In extremely bad conditions, have a flue liner fitted. One of these is in the form of a balloon which is let down the chimney, tied at the bottom and inflated with air to the required dimensions. A preparation is then poured in between liner and old bricks and, when hard, the balloon is deflated and withdrawn.

Sometimes, with an open grate where a slow combus-

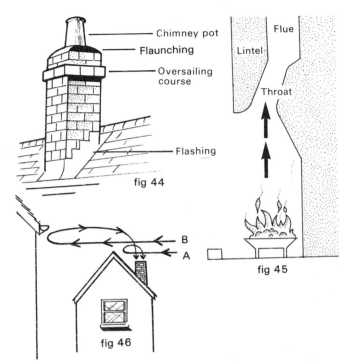

fig 44

fig 45

fig 46

tion stove has been fitted, a chimney will develop a dangerous tilt. This is caused through patent fuels expelling sulphurous fumes which don't rise so quickly as those of house coal. A builder should be called in to remedy this fault.

**Fireplace dimensions** An undesirable increase in height between fire and lintel may be the result of having a low sunken fire installed in place of a raised barred grate.

Experiment with a sheet of metal held at the top in front, raising and lowering it after lighting a fire. When right, fit a cowl of burnished copper or sheet aluminium permanently in position. These can be bought to size and come with fittings. For an average size of grate the lintel

85

shouldn't be much more than 450mm (18in) above the fire, the throat not more than 250mm (10in) wide and 100mm (4in) from front to back; length 200 to 250mm (8 to 10in), see Fig.45. The facings must be smooth and free from jutting out bricks likely to deflect smoke back.

Another cause of smoky chimneys is the stack coming below the level of the ridge roof tiles where reflected wind can blow smoke down, Fig.46A or where a house adjoins a relatively tall building, B. The remedy is to increase the height of the chimney or fit a specially designed cowl.

**Cracked fireback and hearth** Replace with a new fireback which can be bought to fit almost every shape, or, if not too bad, patch with fireclay knifed well in. For wide cracks caulk first with asbestos cord to minimise further cracking.

Tiled hearths crack across the centre through differences in coefficients of expansion between tiles and mortar. One remedy that might help is to lay new tiles on a sheet of plasterboard using a weak tile cement. With a very old hearth you may not be able to replace the tiles to match the surround uprights. A way out of this difficulty is to hack off all the old hearth tiles and trowel on a screed of mortar consisting of one part by volume of cement and four of silver sand. Its greyish colour can be transformed, not with oil paint which will blister nor emulsion which turns brown under heat, but by rubbing with a donkey stone. If you cannot get this stone, use old-fashioned, non-washable distemper (not water paint), or one part by volume of powdered glue size mixed with about sixteen parts of whiting and sufficient water to give a creamy consistency. Brush it on and, when it turns black in patches, redistribute the white by wiping over gently with a wet cloth. Eventually you'll have to wash it all off and replace with new. That doesn't take long. Stone fireplaces can be kept clean with silicate of soda which will last about two years without needing renewal. The colour of the stone may darken slightly during this period.

# 9.INSULATION

In the last century and before, draughts in rooms were taken for granted. Hence winged arm chairs and fireside settles. A change in design of buildings, the absence of open fires and chimneys and installation of small-bore central heating came from a demand for more comfort, paid for by the increasing price of all fuels. This has meant an increasing emphasis on insulation.

**Heat losses** The percentages of heat loss applying to a detached house shown in Fig.47 give only a very rough guide. Large picture windows will throw out the percentages and, if a structure is built entirely of glass, such as might be in a garden, then they make nonsense. If your house is semi-detached, heat loss will be less and, if it's in the middle of a terrace, it'll be less still because you will derive heat from your neighbours' dwellings and they from yours, a sort of communal effort!

**Insulation first** It's common sense to attend to insulation *before* central heating because, once installed, you'll derive its benefits immediately from whatever form of heating is already in existence. Complete insulation is reckoned at about five per cent of the cost of building a new house. If it is carried out afterwards, piecemeal, it will cost more, but a little can be done each year.

**Roof** Start with the attic which costs least and is easily insulated by the most unhandy of handymen. All that is needed is 100mm (4in) of granular insulating material tipped between the attic joists. A better and cleaner way is to buy it in quilted form, cut it to size and lay between the joists. Even more efficient is to drape the quilt over the joists in a complete piece. It should be stressed that

100mm (4in) thickness is needed, anything less doesn't do the job properly. If only half that thickness is already in existence, add to it. Protect your hands while working.

As this will increase cold conditions in the attic, cut an aperture in the quilt wherever there's a water tank; lag the tank by tying insulating quilt round it. Wrap exposed pipes with wide insulating tape sold for the purpose or use moulded polystyrene sections. See that large holes surrounding ill-fitting pipes ascending to the attic are stopped round and check that the attic hatch fits well.

Many people stuff newspaper in the eaves under the impression that this will keep the attic warmer; a mistake because you must have ventilation under roof spaces and fire hazard is increased. If there is no gap under the eaves drill holes 12mm in diameter (½in) at 300mm (12in) centres. The aim is to keep heat in below and the attic well ventilated.

**Walls** If your home is fairly modern it will have cavity walls; that is, an outer sheathing of half-brick, a space of 50-60mm (2-2½in) and an inner lining of, perhaps, building blocks. Still air within the cavity is quite a good insulator, but if there is an opening at the top, as there generally is, the air that is warmed by heat from the room will rise and escape. If there's no such opening, air immediately adjacent to the inner sheathing, being warm, will also rise. The higher it rises the more it will cool and, becoming heavier, drop on the outer sheathing side and rise cold to warm up again, so forming an elongated ellipsis of moving air to dissipate heat. This is shown in an exaggerated form in Fig.48.

Infilling the cavity is a job for an expert, and the operator *must* be expert or you are likely to experience failure. The whole of the cavity must be filled, every inch of it, by pumping insulating material through holes bored in the outer wall. For the average size of house the job will take only a day and the menage won't be upset in the least. Go to a reliable company recommended by the makers of the material. Don't be put off by an operator saying that filling can stop at eaves height; a gable must be filled as well because if, for any reason, damp accumu-

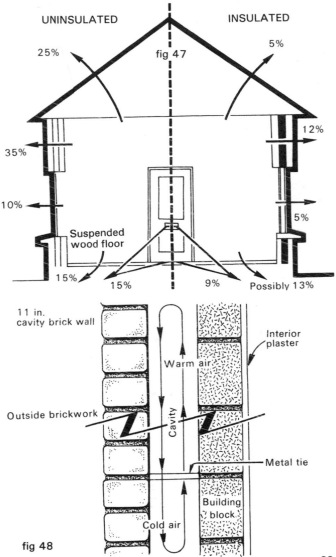

UNINSULATED    INSULATED

25%    fig 47    5%

35%    12%

10%    5%

Suspended wood floor

15%    15%    9%    Possibly 13%

11 in. cavity brick wall

Interior plaster

Warm air

Outside brickwork

Cavity

Metal tie

Building block

Cold air

fig 48

lates in an upper cavity, it'll fall on top of the filling to form an inside damp patch. According to reliable information, the best filling material is mineral wool. Polystyrene beads come next and formaldehyde foam last. It is quite within the realms of possibility that at a future date an even more efficient material may be found than any of these.

**Solid walls** The whole-brick walls of earlier houses have no cavities to fill; but you can decrease loss of heat by nailing 25 × 32mm (1 × 1¼in) studs to the inner side and fixing insulating board on top. The cavity thus created can be infilled if you like, though the fibrous nature of the board will, to an extent, be its own insulator through entrapping still air between the fibres. Size the board before papering or apply alkali resisting primer before painting. This will, of course, decrease the size of what may be an already small room. An alternative, and rather an expensive one, would be to sheathe the outer wall with timber, plastic or tile cladding. Where wood is used, interline with an impervious membrane such as building paper to prevent condensation.

**Floors** Not much can be done with heat dispersal through suspended wood floors except having a good, thick underlay to a wall-to-wall fitted carpet. This is inadvisable with a solid concrete floor because of the fear of 'sweating' which might rot the underlay and result in bad odours. Fortunately, most solid floors retain some ten per cent more heat than suspended ones, though they will feel cold to bare feet. If wood blocks are laid on top of concrete (which, of course, must have an impervious membrane underneath) there will be still less heat loss.

**Draughts** Cold air comes in through badly fitting doors and windows, see chapters on doors and windows. Ensure that the spring on your letterbox functions properly and, as an additional precaution, fix a small piece of rubber or composition sheeting over the inner side of the box. A closed-in porch will do much to prevent draughts through the front door. Fit a weatherboard, Fig.22, page 49, to the bottom of the kitchen door facing directly to the outside.

A gap will appear sooner or later under a skirting-board. Stop this up with 15-25mm (½in) quadrant moulding illustrated in Fig.22, page 48. Nail only to floor, not to floor and skirting alternately or you may miss the skirting in places. Splitting may also develop through structural movement.

**Double glazing** The multitude of advertisements in newspapers and glossy magazines may lead you to believe that double glazing is the solution to all insulating problems; but a glance at percentages given in Fig.47 will show this is not so, and a heavy curtain might be just as efficient, though you can't keep curtains drawn all day long! Double glazing is the most expensive of all insulating projects and therefore should be the last to be considered. Net curtains act as a fair insulator, entrapping still air between the threads.

Permanent hermetically sealed double windows are the best and these are generally installed by agents of the makers. You can buy do-it-yourself units where the hinges of the second pane can be released for cleaning, but these aren't so efficient. Neither are those that fit into window frames. Covering frames with transparent polythene isn't very effective and spoils the appearance of a window. It also tends to attract condensation and mould growth within the gap. Certainly the hazard can be minimised by inserting a small bag of silica crystals but this looks unsightly unless disguised by the edge of a curtain.

The gap between panes should be at least 20mm (¾in), and if you want insulation against outside sound as well the gap should be 100mm (4in). This will not decrease sound from inside as noise in another room is transmitted through walls and floors acting as a sounding board.

One advantage of double glazing is that it makes all parts of a room usable. You can even work or read close to a window without discomfort and it also helps to reduce condensation. Another is that it can be carried out piecemeal, tackling the most used rooms first. This saving will be lost when professionals are called in, for travelling time to and fro more than once will be added to your bill. A claim made by double glazers is that two panes are burglar-proof, but they act only as a deterrent. A thief will have two panes to cut through to reach the window catch and there'll be two lots of falling glass. He can tell whether a window is double glazed or not by shining a torch on the outer pane. The inner one will reflect light back.

**Ventilation** You can never really hermetically seal your home in its entirety. A good job, otherwise you'd be faced with a super-dry and stuffy atmosphere, productive of headaches and sore throats. For a family of four, half the air should be changed each hour. This is normally accounted for by opening and closing room doors; if not, you will have to open the window slightly at intervals. You can buy humidifiers if the room gets too dry.

# 10. WOODWORM AND ROT

Woodworm is prevalent in many old houses; modern ones, in most developed countries, are built with pre-treated timbers. If you live in one of the former, climb into the attic space and, with a powerful hand torch examine every yard of rafters and joists and, if you detect round or elliptical holes 1.5-3mm ($\frac{1}{16}$-$\frac{1}{8}$in) diameter so perfect in construction that no man-made tool could be responsible, then it is likely to be the work of the common furniture beetle. Small piles of frass looking for all the world like splashes of dirty plaster are composed of wood powder that has either passed through the grubs' bodies or been kicked out.

When you have finished your inspection in the attic, examine room flooring, dark cupboards, under stairs and the floor round a water closet pan.

It isn't the beetle that does the damage but the lavae it produces. Eggs are laid on rough wood and, on hatching, the grubs bore through, up and down with the grain for some three years when they come to the surface, pupate and new beetles emerge to lay more eggs.

The holes you see are, therefore, flight holes. Entry holes are so minute that you won't detect them. Don't let a timber merchant deceive you by talking about 'dead' woodworm. The grubs cannot be dead unless you have killed them immediately or caused their death when they emerge by the use of a poisonous woodworm fluid.

**Treatment** The following applies to attic spaces. First, brush down the timbers with a banister brush and clear out any debris deposited on the top part of the top bedroom ceiling, between joists. A vacuum cleaner will help as far as removal of dust is concerned, but make sure that nothing solid is lying about. Electricians and plumbers are notorious for dropping bits of metal and wood wherever they're working.

Then, with nose and mouth protected with a mask, apply a woodworm fluid to the entire timber surfaces, using a two-gallon garden pest sprayer with a hand pump which requires operating at intervals. A paint spray gun is of no use because it emits a fine spray whereas the object is to soak the surface. Garden sprayers have a long, lance-like nozzle enabling otherwise inaccessible parts to be reached without undue stretching. This won't kill the grub already in the wood but it will when the grub emerges, so controlling family expanse. Overspray should be sufficient to deal with laths if the underneath ceiling is of lath and plaster. In the case of a wood and plaster partition wall you will have to brush the chemical on the inside laths as there will be little or no overspray.

Woodworm fluid can be obtained in a quick drying and non-staining grade, but if you get a stain from excess fluid seeping through plaster to the ceiling below, allow the fluid to disperse and dry, and then touch in with aluminium primer sealer before redecorating.

An attic room where the horizontal part of the ceiling won't permit entry above will need a square opening cut to allow you to squeeze through and spray that part. Make a movable chipboard cover to fit over the top of the opening. The sloping parts at each side of the ceiling can be reached with the long nozzle of the sprayer, working from the top down and from the bottom up, Fig.49.

**Floors** Examine floorboards with the same care you have devoted to roofing timbers. If you see any holes they will be the exit of pupated grubs, many of which will still be burrowing in the supporting joists. Rip up every fourth or fifth board, and brush and vacuum out. Then pass the spray nozzle underneath and work on the undersides of the remaining boards you've removed and the joists. Replace the boards and spray the top, Fig.50. As the treated timber may damage some floor coverings, play safe by laying sheet polythene under the covering.

The effectiveness of the fluid is at least twenty to thirty years, not like paraffin or kerosene which is also deadly to

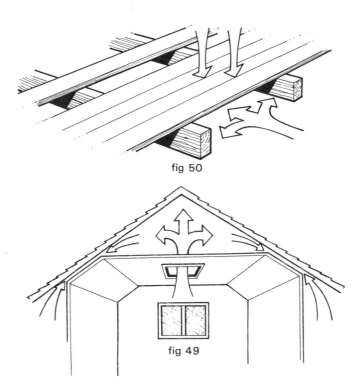

fig 50

fig 49

woodworm but has small lasting powers. It's a good idea to stop up the holes after treatment with a cellulose stopper so that after twenty years when you come to re-examine the timber you can tell at a glance whether or not there's a fresh outbreak.

**Powder post beetle** This is less prevalent than furniture beetle and has a life cycle of only ten months and treatment is the same.

**Death watch beetle** Mostly feeds on dead branches of trees but is sometimes found in house timbers affected by fungus, one of its favourite foods is oak. As flight holes are larger than those of the furniture beetle – at least 2mm (⅛in) – they're easier seen and, being fewer in number, can be injected with woodworm fluid as well as surface-sprayed.

**Longhorn beetle.** There are nearly sixty species of house longhorn beetle with a life span averaging five years. This pest can do ten times the damage of a common furniture beetle but it doesn't as a rule tunnel deeply and so its predations, which are mostly confined to near surface, are more readily seen. Scrape these parts and touch in with woodworm fluid before giving the timbers an all-over treatment. Where an outbreak is extremely bad, the timbers may have to be reinforced.

**Termites** Often called white ants, not because they're of the same classification but because they practise a similar social organisation. They abound in tropical and semi-tropical countries and mostly live underground. Where houses are lifted on stilts to keep a building cool, the insects can climb and attack timber and, for that reason the damp-proof course at the top of the stilt is cut to overhang the edges to discourage but not completely stop them climbing farther. Structural timbers in these countries should be pre-treated.

**Estimating quantities** To estimate how much wood-worm fluid to buy for, say, a boarded roof, take the overall measurement and add twice the depth of a rafter to its width and by the number of rafters. Unboarded: add the width of a rafter to twice its depth; multiply by its length and by the number of rafters. King and queen posts: measure all round and multiply by height. Joists: width plus twice depth multiplied by length and the number of joists.

**Spreading power** Most chemical fungicides: 1 litre = 9 to 11m$^2$ (11 to 13 sq.yds). 1 gallon = 50 to 60 sq. yds.

# Furniture and room trim

Furniture beetle is discouraged by paint, varnish and polish. What it *does* like is rough, uncoated wood; and that is why it is advisable to paint the bottoms of new doors before hanging. The beetles can fly, that is how they colonise in parts of the country not previously infected. But they prefer walking and when they reach the rough, unpainted bottom edge of the door will start breeding. One of the grubs may burrow too high within the timber and, unable to find its way back, force its way through the paintwork of the bottom rail of a door. Don't just be satisfied with treating this but take the door off its hinges and you'll doubtless find it riddled with holes which should be injected with fluid and more fluid applied liberally over the edge.

A similar attack is often found on the outside of a picture rail or skirting-board (base board). Here the beetle climbs behind and lays eggs on the rough underside. If you discover holes in the process of repainting, paint first and inject after the paint is dry because paint doesn't take too kindly to newly applied woodworm fluid. If the rail or board is badly infected, rip it off, burn and renew.

**Furniture** Furniture is generally made of painted or varnished hardwood, and an attack of woodworm is therefore confined to undersides of chairs, insides of drawers and backs of wardrobes which are rougher and uncoated. As most furniture is made of non-absorbent timbers it is of no use carrying out the treatment followed for softwood structural timbers. The holes have to be injected. Woodworm fluid for this type of work is sold in smaller quantities than that required for the large expanse of structural timbers, and each container is provided with a nozzle attachment designed to fit into a hole, but seldom does! Do your best, however, inserting the nozzle in the hole as well as you can and squeeze. The fluid may spurt out of another hole some distance away, showing that the borings are interlinked and therefore treatment need be given only to every fourth or fifth hole. Then brush over the surface with more fluid. Stopping up holes, after treatment, with cellulose stopper would be unsightly. Dabbing over the stopping with paint could look spotty. Furniture polish would soak into the sides of the holes. So try colouring warmed candlewax with pigment of the right tone and then knife that over.

**Wickerwork** The intricacies of wicker furniture may render the reaching of some holes impossible. In very bad outbreaks, therefore, the only safe thing to do is to burn the piece at the bottom of the garden, well away from the house.

# Decay in structural timbers

If a house is built as it should be and properly looked after there is no excuse for rotting wood – a good thing because timber is the most versatile of all building materials and isn't likely to be superseded to any great extent by plastic or metal. In order of frequency, the following are chief causes of faults.

**Surface defibration** The result of a raw surface becoming de-natured by weather, and is often seen in window sills which have not been kept painted. It isn't all that serious and can be remedied by scraping until a firm surface is reached and further depredations prevented by paint.

**Wet rot** A misnomer – a better description would be cellar fungus. This spreads with vein-like hypae. If a skirting-board starts to show unevenness and bulges in places, dig in a sharp-pointed knife and, if it sinks easily, lever off the board and you'll doubtless find strands of hypae at the back. The board should be burned straight away, and the wall behind and a new board treated with a rot-resisting chemical.

**Dry rot** This is most serious and can completely destroy a building if not attended to. Its hypae are thicker than those of cellar fungus and, when massed, produce mycelium or fruiting body of mushroom appearance. After consuming wood in one part the hypae have been known to spread over a 3m (10ft) steel joist to find fresh food. It does this with remarkable rapidity through an ability to carry its own water with it. Hence the name *merulius lacrymans,* flood of tears.

An outbreak generally starts in the joists of a suspended ground floor and is caused by damp conditions and insufficient ventilation, too few or badly placed airbricks; then it affects the floorboards and spreads up the stairs to rooms above. Tackle it in its earliest stages. Lift up floorboards and saw off affected parts some 600mm (2ft) beyond the infection. Burn the rotten bits outside immediately. Don't use them as firewood. Brush the remainder clean and apply two applications of dry rot fluid, back and front and at edges. Clean and spray existing pieces using a garden sprayer.

When replacing the rotten boards with new, arrange for the join to come half-way over a joist. Then you can nail the ends of both planks to the same joist. The joists themselves will have to be attended in the same way, of course. Methods of splicing new to old are shown in Fig.7, page 28. If the join comes in the middle of a large room, it would be well to reinforce it with a brick pillar about 230mm (9in) square standing on the subfloor. Separate the timber from bricks with a piece of bituminous damp-proof course. Make sure the ends of joists don't actually touch outside walls. If they are supported on buried wall plates and the plates have badly gone, call in a builder. When only slightly affected, bore 10mm (⅜in) holes at the top front edge and down at an angle of 45°, spaced at some 230mm (9in) intervals. With a funnel, fill with dry rot fluid. Leave to disperse with the grain and fill again.

## Causes of rot

Fungal decay is the result of damp and bad ventilation. A newly felled tree contains fifty to ninety per cent water. This has to be reduced to some twelve per cent before it's ready for use as sawn planks. If moisture content reaches twenty per cent look out for trouble because fungus spores are almost bound to get a footing and there are countless millions of them floating about in the atmosphere.

Damp reaches the timber of a house in the following ways:

1. By faulty plumbing or a burst water tank. In this event make sure there is plenty of ventilation to dry out surrounding woodwork. Lift impervious floor coverings to assist the drying process.

2. Porous bricks of solid walls. See that pointing between bricks is intact and give the *outside* two generous applications of a silicone waterproofing solution.

3. Cracks in rendered walls. Undercut and patch with new mortar.

4. Cracked gutters and damaged downpipes. Patch up or replace with new.

5. Covered air bricks. See that the vents are poked out whenever redecorating outside. No plants should be allowed to grow immediately in front of air bricks which should be arranged to face one another in opposing walls.

6. Flooring bedded directly in mortar without an impervious membrane underneath. Lift the flooring using a pickaxe, insert a membrane, remortar and lay new flooring.

7. Drain surrounds and concrete steps bridging the damp-proof course. Hack off and insert a vertical damp-proof course before rebuilding.

8. Outside rendering spreading below the d.p.c. Hack this off and repoint the footings.

9. Solid floor laid higher than the d.p.c. An example could be two houses built on a slight slope so that one was lower than the other. The owner of the higher house concreted the narrow passageway in between and in so doing brought the concrete above the d.p.c. of his neighbour's house. The result is a damp wall next door.

10. Mortar droppings in cavity walls. These are the result of careless bricklaying, though it is not always easy to prevent. Wedge a long piece of wood suspended by rope immediately below courses of bricks being laid and lifting it as building proceeds. Take care the wedge doesn't fall to the bottom of the cavity.

11. Mortar droppings on brick ties which hold the inner and outer sheaths of a cavity wall together. Again, faulty bricklaying!

With efficient underfloor ventilation by airbricks facing one another in opposing walls, these faults won't *necessarily* lead to dry rot, provided floorboards and joists aren't allowed to touch any part of the outer walls. If, for some reason, they have to, steep the ends of the timber in a wood preservative or coat generously with bituminous paint. If a floor is solid don't use an all-over impervious floor covering. Rush matting is porous and should give no trouble through 'sweating'.

12. Heaping soil above the d.p.c. Always scrape this clear.

13. Faulty d.p.c. The most serious cause of trouble that can be dealt with only by experts who may advise use of an electro-osmotic process.

Dry rot and woodworm are Nature's way of recycling the life of timber. Man's very existence depends upon a continuous battle with Nature. Let that be your consolation when in the attic cursing the existence of such a wonderful plan!

# 11.DAMP

Damp in houses is more prevalent today than ever before in spite of improved laying of damp-proof courses. It leads to damaged decorations, is not good for health and, through evaporation, keeps interior temperature down, thus wasting fuel.

In modern buildings the damp-proof course (d.p.c.) is at least two brick courses up from ground level. It used to be of overlapping slate, then of a non-ferrous metal and now of bitumen-impregnated felt. The object of the d.p.c. is to stop the passage of moisture from the subsoil which would otherwise rise by capillary attraction. In older houses, the d.p.c. is dangerously near the soil so that mossy growths and plantlife growing immediately in front carries moisture to bridge the interlining and wet the wall above. If you own such a dwelling you should, therefore, take extra care to see that the bottom outside of a wall is kept clear and that a flower bed isn't heaped up against it.

In yet older property there isn't any d.p.c., just bricks so closely knit as not to allow the passage of water. We now call them engineering bricks.

**Condensation** The atmosphere contains moisture and in warm weather the air will expand to hold more moisture. When this decreases in volume through striking against a relatively cold surface, surplus water will be deposited. That is why dew forms on grass and house roofs overnight. That is why single-glazed windows become 'steamed up'. That is also why the outside wall of a room is more affected than an inside one which is relatively warm through house heat.

Bathrooms and kitchens soon get steamed up through the use of hot water, cooking and washing. To minimise this, open windows slightly at top and bottom, the upper opening to allow steam, which is lighter than air, to rise and escape, the lower for fresh air to come in and take its place. If cold weather won't allow open windows there is nothing for it but to install an extractor fan in either window or wall immediately facing the cooking stove in the kitchen. You can also decorate these walls with an anti-condensation paint. With gloss paint or waterproof wallpaper, condensed water will stream down. An example of the kind of problem to be encountered follows.

A suspicious damp patch appeared in the bottom corner of a passage leading to the foot of some stairs. The damp-proof course in the house wall was traced through to the outside half-brick extension wall where there was no d.p.c. The builders of this extension evidently thought that, as the wall stood on the quarry tiles of a floor under a verandah, they were safe. The top of the wall was presumably protected by the roof of the verandah. The outside of the house wall in the vicinity was given applications of a silicone waterproofing solution as a temporary measure to prevent the part underneath from becoming saturated and interior decorations ruined. Silicone solution is colourless and doesn't affect the colour of the bricks.

A few months later the original small damp patch had extended up to ceiling height. This gave a vital clue as to what was happening. The quarry tiles were *not* completely impervious and, although the top of the wall was presumably protected by the verandah roof, rain was beating through. There was no vertical damp-proof course and moisture from underneath and up above were forcing their way through the house wall, as is indicated in Fig.51.

One remedy would have been to saw through the juncture of outer wall and house wall with a brick saw and push in a bituminous vertical d.p.c. A tricky job and one likely to weaken the join of the two walls. Instead 7mm (3/8in) holes were bored in alternate brick courses, half-way through the wall on both sides and downwards at an angle of 45°. These were filled twice through a funnel with a silicone solution formulated for the purpose and obtainable at builders' merchants, Fig.52, and the mouths of the holes sealed with mortar coloured with pigment to match

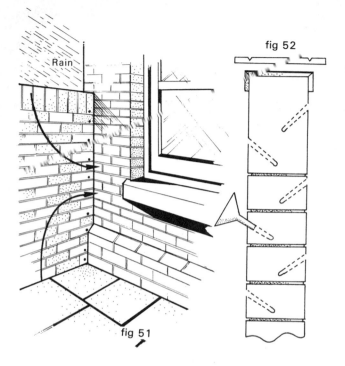

fig 52

Rain

fig 51

the bricks. The theory that the solution would work up and down the porous bricks and stop the ingress of water proved right in practice. The damp patch disappeared altogether.

Strips of bituminous d.p.c. were then scribed to a third of their thickness to allow for bending and the unscribed side coated with mastic compound to act as a sticking agent to the top course of bricks. Capping the top of the wall with ridge tiles might be better but would have increased the cost. The top of the felt was painted with two coats of venetian red bituminous paint so that the addition is hardly discernable.

**Intersticial condensation** With a centrally-heated solid-brick house, cold air may enter the pores of bricks and meet warm air from inside. The result is condensation within the brickwork. Where this meeting point is near the outside, damp will leach outwards and evaporate. But when it meets near an inside surface it will be driven in, causing a damp inner wall, Fig.53. The remedy here is to coat the inside wall with a damp-proofing compound which can be obtained from builders' merchants.

**Brickwork** If your bricks are in doubt, examine the pointing and, if decayed in parts, rake out to a depth of 10mm (⅜in) and patch up with fresh mortar coloured to match the remainder. Where there is extensive deterioration the whole wall will have to be repointed, taking a few feet at a time and attending to the perpendicular joints first and pressing the new mortar well home. Wet the raked-out parts by flicking with a large brush soaked in water, and use a stiff mortar mix to prevent staining the surface.

An application of a waterproofing solution will keep porous bricks dry for at least ten years before needing renewal, but attend to the pointing first.

**Rendering** A crack in outside cement rendering can cause trouble. If you're mystified at a damp patch appearing well *below* the crack, it is caused by the surrounding mortar lifting from the brickwork and water running down in between.

**Roof** Porous cement roofing tiles can be treated with special bituminous compounds made for the purpose. A tile missing from a roof obviously will result in a deluge of water through the ceiling immediately below, Fig.54A. But if only misplaced and causing a mere trickle, the drops could fall on a rafter, run down underneath and drip where it crosses a purlin **B**. Otherwise it will continue until reaching the wall causing dampness at **C**. Or it may run down to the damp-proof course, become entrapped and build up to cause trouble at **D**.

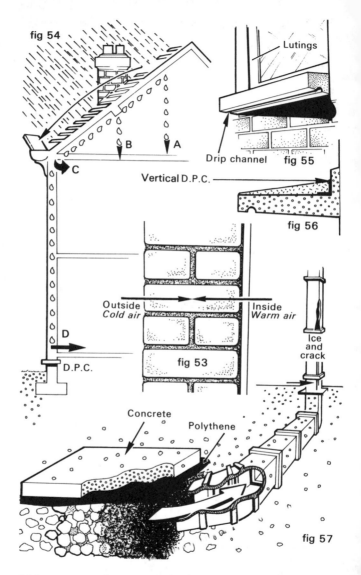

fig 54

Lutings

Drip channel    fig 55

Vertical D.P.C.

fig 56

A

B

C

D

D.P.C.

Outside
*Cold air*

Inside
*Warm air*

fig 53

Ice
and
crack

Concrete

Polythene

fig 57

**Windows** Damp around window frames is likely to be the result of decayed lutings (mortar fillets joining frames to surrounding masonry). The decay may be through structural movement or banging of doors. Close doors quietly, a hearty slam acts like a sledge hammer to a wall, disrupting not only lutings but pointing as well. Rake out the decayed lutings and restop with mastic compound which will give with further movement. Where gaps are wide and deep, pack in nylon cord first to act as a cheap foundation for the mastic.

At the same time look at the drip channel which is near the outside and underneath the sill. Cobwebs and congealed paint often cause rain to run underneath and cause dampness, Fig.55. Tiled sills have a lip at the outside edge to act in the same way as a channel. Check the slope of the sills. If it isn't sufficient, and resetting one of concrete or stone impossible without ruining adjoining brickwork, slightly serrate the top with cold chisel and hammer, brush over with PVA adhesive and mix a little PVA with mortar before screeding over to the correct slope, Fig.56.

**Gutters and downpipes** A leaky gutter can cause a damp patch at the top of a bedroom wall. A cracked downpipe can cause similar trouble in the vicinity of the crack. Iron doesn't crack of its own accord; it will only rust and cause a hole. The crack is the result of a choked sump into which rainwater enters through underground earthenware pipes. In a heavy storm the water, unable to escape through the interstices of the sump, will rise back in the downpipe and, if a heavy frost sets in, ice forms and, in expanding, cause the crack.

Dig near the foot of the downpipe to expose the underground pipes. Trace them along by further digging (you cannot suppose them to run in an invariable straight line) until you reach the sump. Clear out and refill, covering the top with a sheet of heavy duty polythene and adding concrete to prevent overlying soil from falling in and causing further blockage, Fig.57.

Last, scrape rust from the sides of the crack and stop up with plastic metal.

**Broken damp-proof course**   A damp-proof course could crack through subsidence at one side of the house. There is another rare cause, a very heavy frost attacking half the soil immediately below foundations and expanding, whereas the inner half won't be affected. This calls for professional assistance.

# INDEX